DATE DUE

DEMCO 38-296

The Work of Writing

Elizabeth Rankin

The Work of Writing

Insights and Strategies for Academics and Professionals

JOSSEY-BASS
A Wiley Company
San Francisco

350 Sansome St.
San Francisco, CA 94104-1342

www.josseybass.com

Jossey-Bass books and products are available through most bookstores. To contact
Jossey-Bass directly, call (888) 378-2537, fax to (800) 605-2665, or visit our website at
www.josseybass.com.

Substantial discounts on bulk quantities of Jossey-Bass books are available to corpora-
tions, professional associations, and other organizations. For details and discount
information, contact the special sales department at Jossey-Bass.

We at Jossey-Bass strive to use the most environmentally sensitive paper stocks available
to us. Our publications are printed on acid-free recycled stock whenever possible, and our
paper always meets or exceeds minimum GPO and EPA requirements.

Library of Congress Cataloging-in-Publication Data

Rankin, Elizabeth, 1947-
    The work of writing : insights and strategies for academics and professionals /
Elizabeth Rankin.
        p. cm. — (The Jossey-Bass higher and adult education series)
    Includes bibliographical references and index.
    ISBN 0-7879-5679-1 (alk. paper)
    1. English language—Rhetoric—Study and teaching. 2. Academic writing—
Study and teaching. 3. Business writing—Study and teaching. 4. Technical
writing—Study and teaching. 5. Authorship—Study and teaching. 6. Group work
in education. I.
    Title. II. Series.
    PE1404 .R356 2001
    808'.042'071—dc21

                                                                    2001001689

FIRST EDITION
PB Printing   10 9 8 7 6 5 4 3 2 1

The Jossey-Bass
Higher and Adult Education Series

Contents

Preface

Can you recommend a good book on writing? When colleagues ask me this question, I'm never quite sure how to answer. "Writing" is such a broad subject that what one person needs in the way of information, advice, or motivation may be far from what another finds helpful.

Still, it's not an unreasonable question to ask, and I have often wished for a standard title to recommend. If my colleagues are primarily interested in style, I can recommend a couple of good books on that subject. If they are interested in a particular kind of writing (book proposals or scientific papers, for instance), I can offer some suggestions as well. But in many instances what the writer is looking for seems to be something a little different—something that acknowledges the challenges of academic and professional writing yet makes the *work of writing* easier. Or if not easier, then at least more comprehensible, more manageable, and more productive.

What would such a book look like? Ideally, it would focus on the intellectual *work of writing*, that is, on the thinking, strategizing, and decision making that academic and professional writers do. It would also have to deal with the complex issues of purpose, audience, genre, and voice that all writers face.

That's what this book sets out to do.

Although I have organized the book according to themes, it didn't begin with those themes. It began instead as a set of stories that grew out of my experience as a leader and participant in several faculty writing groups over the past several years. Included in these groups have been faculty from disciplines as varied as accounting, anthropology, aviation, biology, chemistry, computer science, counseling, education, English, history, management, medicine, music, nursing, pathology, political science, social work, space studies, Spanish, and theater. Although I have taught writing for over twenty-five years, it wasn't until I began working with these faculty that I realized one important fact: all writers face similar challenges. Whether they are writing a journal article or a grant proposal, a curriculum guide or a consultant's report, the writers in our faculty writing groups tend to raise the same questions, encounter the same obstacles, and offer the same kinds of writing advice. Once I realized this, I knew that telling the stories of *particular* writers working on *particular* projects and getting feedback from *particular* readers would capture experiences common to most academic and professional writers.

In doing so, it would also do justice to the richness and complexity of the writer's work, which is often lost when we try to abstract principles of writing out of the actual contexts in which it occurs. The stories or "scenarios" I present here are all drawn from actual experience. Some are told almost exactly as they happened in our group sessions. In other cases I have merged details from two or more sessions so as to sharpen the focus or bring together related issues. In all cases I have tried to give an accurate sense of the issues that regularly arise and the discussions that occur in our writing groups, changing names and details to keep the identities of the writers anonymous.

One testament to the validity of these scenarios is the fact that in the course of writing this book, I encountered most of the situations and challenges I was writing about.

One of those challenges had to do with defining purpose and audience. In the beginning I imagined this book as a collection of stories that would be both interesting and useful for other academic writers. At that stage the readers I had in mind were faculty and graduate students who wanted to improve their writing and hence their chances of successfully publishing in their fields.

Once under way, however, the project grew in scope. My editor convinced me that what I had to offer would be just as useful for individuals who write in a wide range of professional settings. As I wrote and revised, I worked hard to keep the needs and expectations of this broader audience in mind. And throughout the process I asked myself, "Would my readers see themselves and their own writing in these stories I had to tell? Would they be willing to read a book about writing that worked inductively, drawing general principles from stories, rather than using stories to illustrate general principles?" My own preference for narrative as a mode of sharing knowledge had to be balanced with my editor's sense that many readers desire more explicit organization and advice.

Another challenge had to do with finding the right professional voice. In this case my own preference for an informal, personal style had to be balanced with the conventions of scholarly writing, which favor a more formal professional tone.

Like most writers, I encountered occasional blocks in the course of writing. At various stages I became discouraged, and when interruptions occurred it was difficult to get back on track. Another problem was simply knowing when to stop. Because my own writing group is still meeting weekly, we are continually producing new stories that could enrich the book in any number of ways. But eventually I had to take my own advice and simply "get it in the mail."

Throughout the process I have relied on helpful feedback from others in many ways and at many stages. The original idea for the book came from a conversation with my friend and writing group colleague, Denise, when we formed a summer "writing group à deux." Once I got started I shared my work regularly with Denise, and it was her encouragement and the incentive to have something to show her that kept me writing.

That was in the beginning. In subsequent months I brought draft work to my full writing group (Harmon Abrahamson, Victoria Beard, Anne Gerber, Cindy Juntunen, Melinda Leach, Dan Sheridan, Tom

Steen, and Denise Twohey), and their honest and helpful feedback has been invaluable. I owe them special thanks, not only for reading my work in progress but for allowing me to draw occasionally on their work and on our many conversations over the years.

When I first sent out my book proposal and got a favorable response from Jossey-Bass, I also began getting feedback from a Jossey-Bass senior editor, Gale Erlandson. In fact it was Gale's detailed and insightful comments on the manuscript that helped me make the decision to go with Jossey-Bass as a publisher. My notion of a good editor is one who will tell you what you don't want to hear in ways that can help you hear it, and also one who can hear what you have to say when you push back gently against the suggestions she offers. Gale has been remarkable in both these respects, and the book owes much to her personal interest in this project.

Finally, the book could not have been written without the support of my husband, Tom Steen, who I met in one of our first faculty writing groups and who continues to serve as my in-house editor, adviser, and traveling companion.

Elizabeth Rankin
April 2001

About the Author

Elizabeth Rankin is professor of English and serves as director of the Office of Instructional Development at the University of North Dakota in Grand Forks. She received her Ph.D. degree in English from the State University of New York at Binghamton in 1980. She leads writing seminars and teaching workshops for faculty in all disciplines. Her book *Seeing Yourself as a Teacher* (National Council of Teachers of English, 1994) grew out of her work with graduate teaching assistants in the English Composition Program, and she has published articles on writing and on literature in a variety of professional journals.

Active in several professional organizations, Rankin is also a consultant-evaluator for the National Council of Writing Program Administrators.

She and her husband enjoy camping and canoeing in northern Minnesota and Michigan, as well as long road trips to other parts of the country.

The Work of Writing

1

The Work of Writing

Writing is neither a simple skill nor an inborn talent. It is, as most academics and practicing professionals will testify, a complex intellectual activity that engages us throughout our adult lives. In this respect writing is not unlike the other work we do in professional settings: teaching classes and running seminars, advising students and consulting with clients, working on research projects alone or with peers. Writing can be enormously frustrating at times, but it can also be immensely rewarding.

Like all demanding professional work, writing keeps confronting us with new situations and challenges. In the process of negotiating these situations, we encounter complex ideas, multifaceted problems, and difficulties we have not dealt with before: how to convert *this particular* dissertation into a publishable book, how to persuade *this particular* audience that our proposal is better than a competing one, how to put *this particular* specialized knowledge into language the layperson can understand, how to distill *this particular* concept, which took months to work through, into the mere two hundred words we have been allotted by our editor.

But the very complexity of the writing task is also what makes it rewarding. For writing, just like critical thinking, research, and problem solving, immerses us in the world of ideas. It draws on our creativity, disciplines our thinking, and forces us to engage with those who share our interests and those who challenge our assumptions.

From Graduate Student to Professional

Although there are clearly similarities between the writing we did as graduate students and the writing we do in our professional careers, there are also interesting differences that are not immediately apparent. In graduate school, for instance, writing is often in the form of "school genres" such as the academic essay, the research paper, the lab report, the essay exam—all genres that place the writer in the role of student-novice writing for an audience of teacher-experts. Even the dissertation is a school genre in this respect, though its length may mislead us into thinking of it as a scholarly book. Although some of us were fortunate to have been coached on writing for publication by graduate school mentors, the habit of writing to "show what we know" is not easily shed, as is evident in so much of the writing that fills our professional journals.

Another difference between graduate and professional writing is that in a school context, professors are committed to reading student work. Although they will critique it freely, they cannot simply turn the page and pass over it as a journal reader might. Furthermore, when professors read graduate student work, they are interested not only in the subject but in the intellectual development of the writer. How much has she read? How carefully does he think? How well has she learned the conventions of academic writing?

Once we're out of graduate school and for the rest of our professional careers, we find ourselves writing in very different genres and for very different kinds of audiences. Our readers no longer care about our intellectual development. They are interested only in our subject, and in some cases, even that interest cannot be assumed. In professional settings one of the most important things we learn is how to pose questions for ourselves as writers: What am I trying to say in this piece of writing? Is it something that others have written about before? If so, what is new and important about what I have to say? Or does my saying it in somewhat different language serve a purpose for those who will read it? Will those who do read it have an inherent interest in my subject? Can I count on them to know the background, or must I fill it in? Will they be comfortable with my vocabulary? Am I overexplaining what they already understand? How can I make sure they follow this long, complex argument? Do I need to cut it down to fewer pages? Can I use a more informal, personal voice?

The answers to questions like these are rarely simple, and we are unlikely to find them in writing handbooks or publishers' guidelines. Rather, they require the careful thought and sound professional judgment that we develop and nurture throughout our careers as writers and readers of academic and professional prose.

Taking the Reader's Perspective

In fact it is our experience *as readers* that may be most helpful to us when we set out to write in academic or professional contexts. As readers we are well aware of the kind of writing that floods our professional publications—writing that is dull and lifeless, overly long and boring, poorly organized and jargon ridden. Too often when we begin to write and publish in academic and professional settings, we mindlessly replicate such writing, never stopping to ask ourselves how we might make it clearer, more engaging, more reader friendly. Like new parents who blindly repeat the mistakes of the adults who raised them, we don't take time to question the assumptions behind our behavior. Why begin a scholarly essay with an exhaustive review of literature on the subject? Because that's the way we were told to do it. Why employ so many indirect passive constructions in a scientific paper? Because that's how scientific papers always sound.

Of course, it is not necessary or even possible to question every genre convention, every rule we have been taught to follow. Conventions serve a purpose in writing: they save us from having to reinvent the wheel every time we sit down to compose our thoughts. But conventions also calcify, and imperfectly understood conventions can create huge, unnecessary problems for the writer. For

example, I once had a student who was so fearful of using the pro-
scribed "I" in her papers, as well as the generic masculine "he," that
she went to great lengths to avoid using pronouns altogether, with
predictably disastrous results.

That's why it is important that we be active, observant readers
of published writing in our fields. As readers we can become more
aware of the range of options we have as writers—options that may
be far broader than we realized. We can also become more sensitive
to those features of writing that attract and engage us as readers, as
well as to those that confuse and annoy us.

Lessons from the Faculty Writing Seminars

In this book I promise no quick fixes, no shortcuts, no formulas for
academic and professional writing. Instead I offer a framework to
help writers think about their writing in realistic, practical, and productive ways. It is a framework that draws on the collective experience of academic and professional readers as well as writers and on
the collective wisdom of scholars in the field of rhetoric and writing.

One thing this collective experience and wisdom suggests is that
academic and professional writing is not so very different from other
kinds of writing. Although writers in these settings may produce
different kinds of documents—research reports rather than business
memos, scholarly journal articles rather than newspaper stories, reviews of the professional literature rather than movie reviews—the
way effective academic and professional writers think about their
writing is quite similar to the way successful journalists or novelists
or advertising copywriters think. In fact, every suggestion I offer in
the chapters that follow could be applied, with only slight modifi-
cations, to virtually any writing context.

Still, it is easier to understand how such advice applies when we
see it in our own situations. Along with general principles, we need
specific examples and real-life scenarios to relate to. In this book
the examples and scenarios should be quite familiar to academic

writers and, by extension, to practicing professionals as well. They reflect the concerns of actual writers because they come directly from faculty writing groups I have worked with for several years.

When I first began working with the faculty writing groups (interdisciplinary groups of faculty who meet regularly to read and respond to each other's work), I was struck by how different the things we were writing seemed to be: a scholarly article about theater history, a curriculum proposal for a new chemistry major, a technical analysis of a computer program, a personal narrative illustrating a social work professor's own experience with human service agencies during a natural disaster. How could we find any common ground to talk about? Yet we did. What struck us all immediately when we began reading each other's work was how similar our writing was—how the same themes came up again and again in our comments: "What's your point?" "Who are you writing this for?" "I like your voice." "Can you move that point to the front?" "How about using subheadings to let us know where you're headed?"

Similar too were the themes we heard in each other's writing struggles: the difficulties we all had getting started and the frustrations and blocks we encountered throughout the writing process.

Common Themes

In the chapters that follow, I have compiled several stories from the faculty writing groups that embody those common themes. Generally speaking, they cluster into four related groups:

- *Contributing to the professional conversation:* defining your contribution, getting into the conversation, and maintaining your vision of the whole

- *Meeting readers' needs and expectations:* thinking about purpose, audience, genre, and other aspects of the rhetorical situation

- *Finding your professional voice:* creating a sense of voice in your writing without sacrificing professional credibility

- *Seeing the project through:* getting started, overcoming internal resistance to revising, and getting your manuscript in the mail

These aren't the only issues writers face, of course. But I think they may be the most important issues. Any writer who can be clear about his or her contribution, anticipate the needs of the audience, work within (or sometimes press gently against) expected form and genre conventions, establish a sense of voice, produce a carefully revised manuscript, and actually get it in the mail has an excellent chance of succeeding as a writer.

Writing Groups and Individual Writers

Because the scenarios in this book all derive from situations that arose in our faculty writing groups, it may be useful to say something here about those groups. Although there are many ways to structure a writing group (none inherently better than another), those I have led and participated in have been fairly similar in pattern. For readers interested in starting their own groups, more detailed information and sample materials are included in Appendix A.

When our writing groups meet for the first time at the beginning of the academic semester, we agree to a set of ground rules, and each of us signs up for a date when we will bring a piece of writing-in-progress to the group. It might be a very early draft or a nearly finished piece. It might be a scholarly article, a textbook chapter, a grant proposal, a book review, a newsletter article, or a conference presentation. Whatever we bring, we ask that our colleagues read it in the spirit of helping us make it better. We want them to be our test audience, our screening room. This they can do in three ways:

(1) by telling us what they like and what works for them, (2) by responding to questions we have asked them to focus on, and (3) by giving us additional suggestions and encouragement.

Of course, it is not always possible to assemble a supportive faculty writing group. And even if it were, not everyone is comfortable working in a group context. For that reason this book is addressed primarily to individual writers—academics and professionals—who, like the great majority of writers, usually work alone.

Still, even writers who work alone can gain useful perspective by viewing their writing through the eyes of other readers. For that reason each scenario in this book ends with two sets of suggestions: one set involves "Getting Feedback from Others"; the other is designed for "Writing on Your Own." Although the suggestions in the first set will be especially useful for those who work in writing groups, they should be helpful to anyone who can persuade a trusted colleague, student, or partner to read a draft or serve as a sounding board in the early stages of a writing project.

It is in those early stages, after all, that some of the most important work of writing gets done.

2

Contributing to the Professional Conversation

Consider the following passage from the work of philosopher and rhetorician Kenneth Burke:

> Imagine that you enter a parlor. You come late. When you arrive, others have long preceded you, and they are engaged in a heated discussion, a discussion too heated for them to pause and tell you exactly what it is about. In fact, the discussion had already begun long before any of them got there, so that no one present is qualified to retrace for you all the steps that had gone before. You listen for a while, until you decide that you have caught the tenor of the argument; then you put in your oar. Someone answers; you answer him; another comes to your defense; another aligns himself against you, to either the embarrassment or gratification of your opponents, depending upon the quality of your ally's assistance. However, the discussion is interminable. The hour grows late, you must depart. And you do depart, with the discussion still vigorously in progress. [Burke, 1941, 110–111]

When Burke used this metaphor to describe what he called the drama of human interaction, he had more in mind than academic conversations. But for those of us working in academic and professional contexts, the metaphor seems particularly apt. In many ways the books and articles that fill our professional journals and publishers' catalogs are like these "parlor conversations," with each discipline or profession conversing excitedly in one part of the room.

As writers our first obligation is to think about what we are contributing to that conversation—what new information, insight, theoretical perspective, argument, application, approach, or deepened understanding we have to share with others in our field. As we write and revise, it is vitally important to stay focused on that contribution and to make sure that our readers stay focused on it as well.

For our writing to be effective, there is probably nothing more important than this. Yet in the faculty writing groups I work with, it often proves surprisingly difficult.

Scenario 1: Defining Your Contribution

For Sara, two years out of graduate school, the challenge is how to publish something from her lengthy dissertation, which was a detailed analysis of the work of a contemporary playwright. Her adviser, who had liked one particular chapter, has urged her to revise and submit it to a journal that is planning a special issue on the topic.

Because she is having trouble getting started on the project, Sara sets a deadline for herself to bring a draft to our faculty writing group. She knows the piece is too long, she says, but perhaps we can help her cut it.

When we meet to discuss the draft, we begin by doing what Sara asked us to do: editing wordy sentences and chopping paragraphs here and there. When someone suggests radically shortening the literature review section, another member of the group speaks up. He had trouble, he says, determining where the lit review left off and Sara's own ideas began. Could she explain a little for us?

For Sara, it turns out, that is not an easy task. The theory she is applying to the playwright's work is actually a well-known scholar's theory. And that scholar recently published a book in which he discussed some of this work as well. When Sara wrote her dissertation, the study had not been published. Now that it has been, her own work feels less original, even to her.

For a while there is silence in the room. We are feeling bad for Sara and she is feeling terribly discouraged. Then someone says, "So this guy stole your idea and got there first, eh?" and Sara says, "Yes, unfortunately." Then, almost as an afterthought she adds, "Well, not *exactly* my idea."

In the ensuing conversation Sara explains that the well-known scholar has not done a detailed analysis of the plays. He just mentions them as examples that illustrate his theory. "What I do is use his theory to do a detailed analysis of three plays," she says. "One of them is fairly well known—the play that won the Pulitzer. The others are more obscure, but they are interesting in their own right. When you read them through the lens of this theory, they are far richer and more complex than they may appear."

Again there is silence in the room, but this time it is because we are all thinking about what Sara has just said. "Can't you just say that?" someone finally asks.

"I thought I did," says Sara. But when we go back through the draft, none of us can find a passage that spells out Sara's point so clearly and succinctly. Before we leave for the day, she asks us to help her remember what she just said; she writes it down in exactly those words.

When we next see Sara's paper, it is both shorter and more clearly focused. She has kept the most pertinent references to other critics and given due credit to the well-known scholar's book. But whereas the first version tended to blur the boundary between that scholar's work and her own, this revised version uses his work as a critical jumping-off point. We no longer have to wonder where his work ends and hers begins.

At the beginning of a writing project, writers usually have a good sense of what they are setting out to do. They have researched the subject thoroughly, read what has been written about it, and thought carefully about how their ideas and findings relate to those of others. As the writing goes on, however, it is not at all unusual for writers to lose focus and forget their original intentions. Actually, this is perfectly natural, for as psycholinguists have demonstrated, the relationship between thought and language is extremely complex. We don't simply think, then speak or write. Rather, our speaking and writing are forms of thinking—processes of discovery in themselves.

Sometimes this process of discovery can be a very positive experience, leading us to see connections and relationships we had not seen before. In other instances, however, the writing process can lead us away from our original intentions, blurring our focus and causing us to lose sight of our own contribution to the field.

One thing that can easily discourage academic writers is the sense that what they have to offer is no longer new or original, and this is one sense in which the conversation analogy can be helpful. Clearly, there is no point in simply repeating what others have already said about a given subject, but that doesn't mean each speaker must introduce a new topic. Writers are perceived to be making useful contributions to the conversation in their disciplines when they expand on or clarify what others have said, offer alternative perspectives, or make connections with related subjects.

In Sara's case her contribution affirmed the usefulness of an idea that another scholar had contributed by showing how it could illuminate a topic few had written about previously. However, even if the plays she was interested in were well known and frequently mentioned in the literature, her analysis would constitute a useful contribution if it made a connection others had not yet made.

Another complicating factor can be the writer's level of confidence. Although some writers are eager to join in the conversation in their disciplines, others hang back, nodding at what previous scholars have said and whispering in muted voices that are difficult to hear. This may have been the case with Sara. Because of her admiration for the well-known scholar whose work she was drawing on, she could not quite imagine herself "interrupting" the conversation to get her own point across. Although the work she had done had clearly earned her a place in the conversation, she could not yet see herself in that distinguished company.

Getting Feedback from Others

In our faculty writing groups, we often ask the writer to explain what is new about the work he or she is doing. In most cases the explanation is very helpful, even though it doesn't appear anywhere in the paper itself. In these instances we urge the writer to "write that exactly the way you said it just now."

Unless your readers come from your discipline, you can't expect them to know whether what you have to say will be regarded as news by others in the field. But you can ask them to read your draft and give you some helpful feedback.

- If you think you have made your point clearly but just want to make sure, ask your readers to put an asterisk next to the passage that they believe captures the gist of what you are saying. If all or most of your readers agree (and if you agree with them), you know you're on the right track. If only one reader out of several misses the mark, it may be that reader's problem, not yours. But if several intelligent readers identify several different "main ideas" in your writing, you probably have some additional work to do.
- If you're in the early stages of the project and are having trouble figuring out where you're going, ask your writing group, a colleague, or a friend to just talk it through with you. Describe what attracted you to the topic, how you started working on it, what you learned as you did your research and background work. As you talk, have your listener (or listeners) take notes on what you say and then try to come up with a clear articulation of the main ideas.

- If you have a draft prepared but fear you may have wandered off course, ask your readers to see if they can write down, in their own words, what the central point is. If they miss it, tell them what you were trying to do and ask them why it didn't come across.
- In the cases described, the idea is to come away with a sentence or two that sums up what you want to say. When you go back to your study, try writing the key sentence out on a note card and posting it above your computer or writing desk. Later, if you lose your way again, glance up at the sentence and read it aloud to yourself. Use it as your compass, and you may find your way out of writing difficulty.

Writing on Your Own

If you don't have the luxury of a writing group to work with, or if your deadline is looming and there is no time to ask a friend to read your draft, you can train yourself to see your work as others see it.

- Before you begin to write, jot down your central idea: the point, the gist, the angle, the insight, the argument—whatever got you excited enough to want to write this piece. Keep what you have written posted above your computer or writing desk and refer to it often. Revise it if necessary.
- If you discover that you can't really name the central idea in the beginning, that might not be a problem. Perhaps you would say, as novelist E. M. Forster is quoted as saying, "How can I know what I think until I see what I say?" If so, don't worry about having the central idea defined when you start out. Just start writing. After a while, you may find that the idea emerges, unlooked for. All you need to do is recognize it when it comes.
- Instead of sitting at your desk or computer, try writing in a personal notebook or journal for a while. Use a comfortable voice rather than striving for an academic or professional voice, and write about what drew you to this topic or area of research. If you can find a way to say it to yourself informally, it shouldn't take too much work to translate your ideas into more formal language.

- But what if it doesn't come? What if, like Sara, you find that you have written a six- or sixteen- or twenty-six-page draft that still feels unfocused and confused? First, don't be surprised. Professional writers regularly report having to throw out whole drafts and start over from scratch. Your best move at this point is to set the project aside. If you can afford to do it, let it rest for a week. If you are trying to meet a deadline, you may have to settle for an hour or two. The important thing is to *not think about it.*

- When you come back to your desk, don't reread what you have written. Open a blank screen or get out a clean sheet of paper and write: "What it all boils down to is this: _____." Then fill in the blank, in one sentence if you can. Now open up your completed draft and see if this sentence, or one like it, appears there. If it does and if it's near the beginning, that's good. If it's buried in the middle, move it forward. And if you can't find it anywhere, put it in. Your future readers will thank you.

Above all, it's important to trust your intuitive sense that *there is something here worth writing about.* If it was interesting enough to get you started writing, it is likely to be a subject worth pursuing.

Scenario 2: Getting into the Conversation

Although a clear sense of focus is crucial, it does not guarantee that others will read or value our work. Therefore, one of the most important things every writer needs to learn is how to get into the conversation in his or her field.

For those writing on a topic of current interest or responding to a recently published book or article on a given subject, finding an opening in the ongoing conversation may be fairly easy. But what if you are trying to introduce a topic that others in your field aren't familiar with? Or what if you are working in an area that people tend to resist or devalue? In this case the question becomes how to interest readers in your topic, how to persuade them that what you have to say is worth their time and attention.

When Eric began work on his current project, he knew he might have trouble getting it published. That's because both his research topic and his methodology fall outside the mainstream of his discipline. However, Eric sees this as a great opportunity. If he can get published, he will be breaking new ground, establishing himself early in what could be a hot new field of research. So far though Eric has not had great success in getting others interested in his research area. Two editors have returned his manuscript with lukewarm reader reports. One reviewer, who was unfamiliar with qualitative research methodology, complained that Eric's sample size was too small. The other dismissed his topic as "narrow."

When he brings the reviewer comments to the writing group, Eric is understandably discouraged. He knows his topic is important and his methodology sound, but he also knows he is going against the grain of his professional journals. "If you're an established name, they'll publish anything you write," he says, "but if you're unknown, you're better off playing it safe."

What would that mean in this case? Eric himself isn't sure. He can't suddenly broaden his "sample," run statistical correlations, and satisfy the one reviewer, nor is he optimistic about convincing the other that his topic has rich implications for the field. Maybe he should just send it to a lesser journal and hope it gets a better reception there.

At first we find ourselves agreeing with Eric. Perhaps his study is not a good match for this journal, and we all have encouraging stories to tell of articles that were rejected by one editor, only to be accepted by another. Still, Eric is reluctant to give up on this particular journal. Not only is it more prestigious but he thinks his work really belongs there. Despite the one reviewer's skepticism, he is convinced that his topic is relevant to larger issues in the field, and the editorial statement says the journal welcomes research in a wide variety of methodological traditions.

When we hear this, we start asking Eric more questions. Does he read this journal regularly? Have they published qualitative studies before? Not that he can recall, he says, though the editorship has recently changed, and there is one prominent qualitative researcher on the new reviewer board. "What is *her* work like?" we ask. Maybe if he brings in something she has published, we can see what she did differently.

As it turns out, Eric doesn't need our help to learn something from the comparison. One significant difference is in the methodology section, where the other researcher takes some time to explain her choice of methods, showing how her research can deepen and enrich what has already been learned using more traditional methods in the field.

But the biggest difference is probably in the introduction to her study. She begins, as Eric did, by identifying a research question and citing relevant work in the field. But unlike him, she also uses the introduction to explain the significance of her work. Although it focuses on a tiny segment of the population, the introduction reveals some things about that population that raise questions other researchers will find interesting. When Eric sees this, he realizes that he has made a similar argument but not so explicitly and not until the discussion section at the end of his article. To create an opening in the conversation, he needs to establish the significance of his research earlier, connecting it to the ongoing conversation and to questions his readers see as important.

Some people may be reluctant to accept the notion that academic and professional writers have to strategize in order to be heard. If the writer does his research and supports his claims with evidence, shouldn't his arguments stand on their own merit? In an ideal world perhaps they would, but this isn't an ideal world. Editors and manuscript reviewers, like the rest of us, are busy people. They may not have time to read thoroughly every manuscript that comes across their desks. And unless the purpose and significance of a piece of writing is clear from the outset, they may not have the patience to keep reading.

For writers like Eric who want to shift the focus of conversation in their fields, the challenge of getting heard is even greater. It doesn't work to simply interrupt and change the subject altogether. You have to look for an opening or make one for yourself, usually by finding creative ways to connect your own work to questions that interest others in the field.

Getting Feedback from Others

If you expect your intended audience to be resistant or uninterested, it is especially important to get readers who can help you strategize.

- If you haven't submitted the piece yet, tell your colleagues you need them to read from the perspective of the skeptical audience. Chances are they will need some preparation for this role, and it will be your job to help them. Once you have explained the possible sources of resistance, ask them to assume the role of the intended audience, marking passages where they react negatively as they read.

- If the resistance you're facing comes in the form of reviewer feedback, bring in the comments and ask your colleagues to help you respond to them.

Writing on Your Own

It is often said that the best conversationalists are good listeners. And this is just as true of academic and professional conversations as of social ones. Whether you listen literally, by attending professional conferences and participating in research colloquia, or figuratively, by reading widely in your field, it is vitally important to know what others are saying. If you are a careful listener, paying attention not only to big ideas but to the subtleties and nuances of others' voices, you will undoubtedly hear things that relate to the work you are doing. Then your task is to draw out those connections, making them explicit in your writing.

Scenario 3: Maintaining Your Vision

In casual conversation it usually isn't necessary to have a complete sense of what you want to say before you begin to speak. In academic and professional contexts, though, it is important that the writer have a vision of what he wants to accomplish. This means more than doing careful research on the subject. It means having a sense of the whole project and an appreciation for any obstacles that may stand in the way.

Nick and Colleen are working on a textbook for a class they have both been teaching regularly for several years. The original idea for the book came from Nick, who always finds it hard to work with existing textbooks in this area. Often he finds himself assigning chapters but never discussing them in class, and the best moments in his classes seem to come from activities he has designed.

When Nick first suggests to Colleen that they coauthor an alternative textbook, Colleen is skeptical. But after a particularly frustrating semester in which nothing seems to have worked in her section, she decides Nick is right. They do need to write their own book.

The big question for both Nick and Colleen is how to get started. Colleen wants to contact a couple of publishers first to see if anyone will be interested. Nick says it's too early for that. He suggests that they write up what they have been doing, test it out in their own classes this semester, and have something to show a publisher next summer.

Because it was Nick's idea to start with, Colleen agrees to go along with his plan. To divide up the work, they decide that Nick will draft an introduction to the textbook and write the first major chapter. Colleen will work on another chapter and gather some supplementary readings that they can include.

As the semester progresses, Nick and Colleen meet occasionally to compare notes on their classes and update each other on their work. They set a deadline of mid-January to have completed drafts to show each other and make a few notes for future chapters as well.

By the time January rolls around, they are feeling committed to the project. The writing has gone well for both of them, and they are eager to read each other's draft material. When they do, however, they see that problems have arisen.

Nick's introductory chapter comes as a surprise to Colleen. It is far more theoretical than she had imagined and much broader in scope. Does Nick really think they need to cover all these approaches to the subject? The slim, practical handbook she has been seeing in her mind would have to triple in length to include all this material.

Nick sees no problem with what Colleen has written, but the task of writing the introduction has made him take a broader view of their subject area. The course they teach may work fine for them, he thinks, but it won't work for every teacher. Their former colleague Donald, for instance, wouldn't even consider using a text like this one. If they want their text to sell, they will have to consider a much wider audience.

For a while Nick and Colleen seem to be at a stalemate. With a new semester just getting under way, they decide to put the text idea on the back burner and come back to it during the summer.

Meanwhile, however, it is Nick's turn to bring something to the faculty writing group. When he signed up for this date, he expected to have nearly finished versions of the chapters he has been working on, but now the whole project seems to have stalled. When he distributes copies of the introduction, he includes a cover sheet that explains the situation, alluding to the conflict between Colleen and himself. He doubts that we can solve the problem in this case, but at least we can see what we think of the chapter.

When the group meets, we begin with our routine first question: "Does everyone understand what we're reading here? Any questions we need to clear up before we can respond to the piece?" This time, it turns out, there are many questions. What kind of class is the text intended for? How is it different from the text you're using now? Why would a teacher be attracted to the approach you're taking? What are the other chapters going to be? Will there be a separate book of readings, or will they be built in? Are the sample assignments the heart of the text or just examples of the kinds of assignments teachers might use?

Finally someone says, "You probably answered all these questions in your book proposal. Maybe you could just give us that."

"OK, but first we need to write it!" says Nick. He still sees the publisher's proposal as something that comes later in the writing process.

We understand Nick's reluctance to talk with publishers at this point, but we still think a proposal would be worth writing, especially in a collaborative project like this one. Just writing the proposal will force Nick and Colleen to deal with some crucial issues that might not come up otherwise, and having to compare the book they are proposing to other books on the market will help them define their focus more clearly.

When we put it this way, Nick can see the point. He decides to call Colleen this week and suggest that they get together and draft a proposal that makes sense to both of them. They may be able to save the project if they do more planning up front.

At first glance this scenario seems to highlight the difficulties of collaborative writing. And there is no doubt that those difficulties are present. Collaborators may begin with a common sense of purpose but soon find themselves moving in different directions, sometimes because of intellectual differences but just as often because of different work habits and personal styles—not unlike a couple who come to the party together but get involved in separate conversations and lose each other in the crowd.

But the basic problem here has less to do with collaboration than with a problem all writers share: the need to think about fundamental issues in the initial stages of a writing project.

For Nick and Colleen the fundamental issues had never really been discussed. They wanted to write a textbook that instructors could use in a course like theirs, but that was as far as they had gotten in the conceptualizing process. What would be the basic rationale for the book; that is, what features would distinguish it from others? Who would be likely to use it? Would it have a broad enough appeal? As they wrote, it became clearer and clearer that they had conflicting assumptions about some of these questions. And the conflicts weren't just between the two coauthors. They were within each individual as well.

One piece of advice commonly given to writers is to outline a project before they begin working on it. That's not bad advice, though it oversimplifies the relation of thought to language. Because many of us do our thinking and writing simultaneously—unable to know what we think until we see what we say—outlining before writing is not always a reasonable option. And even writers who like to work from outlines may run into trouble of the kind Nick and Colleen faced. That's because the conventional outline focuses attention on organization at the expense of more fundamental issues.

Although the outline Nick and Colleen were working from sketched out a basic structure for their textbook, it left unanswered some important questions that might have been addressed in a book proposal. The form of such a proposal may vary from one publisher to another, but the basic idea is to get the writer thinking about fundamental questions like these: What is the target audience of the book? What is the rationale behind it? What kinds of competing books are already on the market? What niche will this book fill?

From the publisher's perspective the proposal is a useful screening device. Like the pre-proposal process in a major grants program, it helps the publisher or sponsor determine which projects may be worth pursuing, that is, which are likely to repay the investment of time, money, and attention that they will require. From the writer's perspective it is useful for other reasons. By addressing such questions early in the process, writers are forced to see their work in its larger rhetorical context, which may save them considerable time and intellectual energy later on.

Getting Feedback from Others

Starting a major writing project is a little like preparing for a political debate. You need to know your stuff, but you also need to be able to think about it from the perspective of others. And you especially need to anticipate objections and reasons for rejection. This is where test readers can be especially helpful.

• If you're involved in a large project such as a book or a grant proposal, plan on writing a proposal in advance of the actual project. Even if you don't know yet exactly where you will submit the book or grant, draft a short pre-proposal that will answer the basic questions any publisher or funding agency is likely to ask. (See Appendix B for one example of a fairly typical set of book proposal guidelines.) Once you do make a decision about where to submit your work, it should be relatively easy to adapt the generic proposal to the specific questions the publisher or sponsoring agency wants you to address.

• Once you draft a generic proposal, ask a friend or writing group to play the role of the intended audience. Tell them as much as you can about the publisher or sponsor, and make copies for them of any guidelines you have been given. If you want really constructive feedback, ask them to play devil's advocate with the proposal, keeping an eye out for anything that might cause the publisher or sponsor to reject it. At this stage it is still early enough to reconceive the project if you need to.

Writing on Your Own

If you're working on a journal article, review, or report, you probably won't be asked to submit a proposal beforehand. Still, it can be useful to think in terms of a proposal, even when you're starting a shorter project.

- If you're working on a scholarly article, imagine that you are writing a proposal to a particular journal. First, ask yourself some questions: What is the article about? What contribution does it make to the field? What will be its basic structure? Who are you trying to reach with it? Why is it appropriate for this particular journal? Then try writing a one-page memo to yourself, detailing the answers to these questions; keep it close by as you write.

- If you're writing a report, imagine writing the proposal to the person who has commissioned it. What is the purpose of this report? Who will read it and for what purposes? What can they expect to learn from the report? What kind of response would you like?

- Regardless of the project you're working on, imagine questions that are key to that particular project. Then jot answers to those questions in a memo directed to yourself. If they're good questions, and if your answers are clear and succinct, you may find yourself using this material later when you write a cover letter to accompany the final written project.

Working with a Collaborator

In many academic and professional contexts, collaboration is not the exception but the norm. In the writing groups I've worked with, we rarely have two members working together on a project, but we have reviewed work that half of a collaborative team brings in for us to read. In some cases our colleague has been in conflict with a coauthor, and we have tried to offer support. In other cases we've been able to mediate conflict by helping our colleague understand where his coauthor might be coming from. Or we may help him smooth out and blend together a chapter that reads like a pastiche of styles.

If you are working on a collaborative project, your first obligation is to your coauthor, but that doesn't mean you can't use feedback from others as well. Here are some suggestions:

- If you sense conflict brewing between yourself and your coauthor, suggest a time-out from writing to talk through the project together. It's always best to do this sooner rather than later, before anyone has too much invested in a particular approach to the project.

- Learn to recognize where your coauthor has a strong investment and where she might be more easily persuaded to see your point of view. For instance if she plans to include several references to her thesis adviser's work, she may be doing it out of professional loyalty. Or she may be doing it simply because it's the work she is most familiar with. If you prefer to cite someone else's work, you need to know how strongly she feels about the matter.

- If you begin to lose faith in the project, do a little "cost-benefit analysis." Make a list of all the strengths you bring to the project. Then list the strengths your coauthor brings that will make it better in the long run. If the benefits outweigh the costs in time and mental energy, hang in there. If they don't, it may be time to consider a split.

- If you want feedback on a collaboratively written piece, ask your coauthor if he or she would mind your sharing the project with a colleague or writing group. If your coauthor is uncomfortable with doing that, you probably need to talk to each other more first.

- When you bring a coauthored piece to a group or a colleague, ask for comments that you can share with your coauthor. (If you have a writing group, you might even designate a chair at the table for the absent writer.) This way, both you and your colleagues can be positive and constructive instead of blaming your absent coauthor for problems in the writing.

Effective academic and professional writing is writing that makes a significant contribution to the ongoing conversation in the field. For the writer this means defining what you have to say and saying it clearly, concisely, and early enough that the reader cannot miss the point. It also means doing a certain amount of professional strategizing: looking for (or creating) an appropriate opening in the conversation and having a positive, persuasive vision of how your work fits into the big picture.

3

Meeting Readers' Needs
and Expectations

In a classic and influential essay addressed to writing teachers, Wayne Booth argues that all good writers have one thing in common: they know how to adopt and maintain a "rhetorical stance" (1963, p. 141). By this he means that they focus not only on what they are writing about (the subject) but on why they are writing (the purpose) and on whom they are addressing (the intended audience). In Chapter Two the scenarios illustrate one important aspect of this balanced rhetorical stance: the need to be clear about purpose, about what the writer has to contribute to the ongoing conversation in the field. But if a clear sense of purpose is crucial to the writer, just as important is a keen sense of audience. Who will be reading this piece of writing? What will they be looking for? How does the writer take readers' needs and expectations into account without compromising his or her own intents and purposes or the obligation to do justice to the subject?

In some professions, especially those that deal directly with the public, it may be second nature for writers to keep their readers in mind. In these situations excesses of audience awareness can result in a certain kind of rhetorical imbalance that sacrifices content to delivery. Booth calls this "the advertiser's stance" (p. 143). In most academic circles, however, writers tend to err on the other side of the balance, focusing so intently on content that they ignore the relationship of speaker and audience. When this happens, says Booth, what results is "the kind of writing that soils our professional journals" (p. 141).

As readers of those journals, we all know what Booth is talking about: scholarly articles that seem to make a virtue of specialized vocabulary and convoluted arguments, essays that jump from one point to the next as if expecting us to read the writer's mind, or dense proposals that seem written on the assumption that we have nothing better to do than spend hours learning about the writer's favorite research topic. As writers, we all hope not to produce that kind of writing. Yet we often find ourselves falling into it, conditioned by habits we have picked up in graduate school or from reading our professional journals.

How do we break those writing habits? Booth would say we do it by learning to think rhetorically, that is, by keeping in mind the simple fact that writing is "a job to be done for a particular audience" (p. 141). Although the habit of thinking rhetorically may take time to acquire, the good news is that, once learned, it is almost impossible to break.

Scenario 1: Creating Signposts and Roadmaps

One of the ways writers show consideration for readers is by creating signposts that show where an argument is headed. In academic and professional writing these signposts may take the form of thesis statements, forecasting paragraphs, subheadings, and clear transitions. For the most part they are not hard to construct and can be enormously helpful to readers trying to make their way through complex academic texts.

The first time Max brought his project to the writing group, it was a mass of disorganized information. This time it's starting to look like a journal article, but Max wants to make sure it hangs together. On his cover sheet he asks us to give special attention to the relationship between the three major sections and to the way they fit together as a whole.

The first thing we notice when we read through the draft is that Max does a nice job of leaving signposts for the reader. Each of the three sections of the article is clearly labeled with a short subheading that describes the content of the section, and several of us mention how much we like that. When we start to talk about the piece in more depth, though, it turns out that the subheadings may not be adequate.

"I got lost between the second section and the third," one person says. "It almost feels as if you're starting a new paper in that final section. Did I miss something?"

As Max starts to explain the connection, our first response is a fairly typical one.

"Why don't you say that in the paper?" someone says. "It would help make that transition much smoother."

But in this case making smoother transitions doesn't solve all the problems either.

"I can see how you get from section two to section three," says another colleague. "I just don't see why you need section two at all. What would happen if you simply dropped it?"

For a while Max tries to respond to everyone's questions and objections, but every time he explains one thing, something else gets confused. Finally, he says he wants to take the paper back and work on it some more. "I really think both sections are important," he says, "but I clearly haven't explained the relationship between them well enough."

The following week Max brings in a new introduction that he went home and wrote immediately after our session. For the most part it looks like the previous intro with a few significant changes. First, Max has changed the wording of his thesis to reflect the wording he uses later in the paper. Second, he has added a short forecasting paragraph—two sentences that preview where his argument is headed and help the reader see the structure of his essay in advance.

"This is great," says the reader who had advised dropping the second section. "Now that I see where you're heading with this, it falls into place after all. I don't know how I could have missed it the first time."

One reason we couldn't see the connections in Max's argument was that we didn't know where to look for them. For us, reading through this long, complex paper was like trying to follow a friend's car when you don't know where he is headed. If you can stay close to him, all you need is to watch for turn signals—those transitions we were urging Max to improve. But if you have to stop at a traffic light and get too far behind, you can't see his turn signals anyway.

In cases like that it's good to have a map, as well as a sense of your destination. This is what Max provided with his forecasting paragraph, and that's why it solved his readers' problems more easily than we had imagined.

In addition to the forecasting paragraph, there are many other ways of guiding the reader through a piece of writing. In this book I have used my opening chapter to preview the themes the reader will encounter throughout. But I have used a variety of other techniques as well. Sometimes the signposts are fairly obvious, as in the chapter titles, numbered and titled scenarios, and repeated sections called "Getting Feedback from Others" and "Writing on Your Own." Common transitional expressions like *however, furthermore, in addition,* or *another way* will also serve to signal the alert reader. Other signposts, sometimes called *echo links,* are less obvious because they are embedded in the language.

To see how echo links work, step back and look at the paragraph that introduced the last scenario. In the first sentence I have chosen words and phrases that deliberately echo language used earlier in the chapter. Although the phrase "show consideration for the reader" doesn't appear exactly anywhere else, it closely echoes language like "the needs of the intended audience" and "ways that readers can hear and follow" in the introduction to this chapter. The repetition of "signpost" has a similar effect. In the first sentence, "creating signposts" echoes exactly the language of the scenario subheading. At the end of the examples the metaphor shifts just slightly from signposts to maps and turn signals. In the last two sections, two of these terms are used again, reaffirming the points that have been made before.

Getting Feedback from Others

One reason writers don't provide maps and signposts for readers is that they have to feel their way through the text as they are writing. Even those who write with outlines can find themselves veering off course from time to time. By the time the first draft is complete, the writer may be so pleased to be finished that she forgets to look back and see if she has left a map for readers to follow. This is why it's always good to get others to read early drafts.

- When you share your draft with a friend, a colleague, or your writing group, ask readers to note any place where they get lost or have to stop to reread. Don't ask them to tell you how to solve the problem. You'll be able to figure that out. Just have them show you where signposts are needed.
- Another idea is to ask your readers to try to draft a simple outline of the piece. If their outlines look like yours, you've made the structure of your piece clear; if not, check to see what they missed or misinterpreted. Maybe a revised forecasting statement or a simple signpost could solve the problem.

Of course, how to use reader feedback is still the writer's decision. In an early draft of this chapter I began with a quote from Booth's essay that mentioned "the three elements that are at work in any communication effort" (p. 141). A few sentences later I listed three slightly different elements. And then the chapter went on to include five scenarios. Several members of my writing group found this confusing—and with good reason. Apparently I had erected "accidental" signposts pointing in several different directions.

To correct the problem one reader suggested making the signposts more explicit, using the last sentence of the opening section to preview the five scenarios in the chapter. It was a reasonable suggestion, but in this case I chose not to use it. Because these scenarios overlap to some extent, it is not always possible to name a distinct principle that each of them illustrates. Instead of adding more explicit signposts, I went back and removed the misleading ones. What remains is an introduction that gives a general preview of issues in this chapter without naming specific issues that come up in the separate scenarios.

Writing on Your Own

Even with no outside readers, you can develop techniques for guiding readers through your work. If you were lucky enough to have learned in school the importance of good transitions and topic sentences, you may have a bit of a head start on this. But composition teachers—perhaps because they work with shorter papers—often neglect the importance of graphics and subheadings.

- If you're working within conventional frameworks, some of the signposts are already provided for you. Simply labeling sections "Results" or "Discussion" is one way to indicate to readers what they should expect to find in the paragraphs that follow.
- If the section headings aren't given, you can invent them for yourself. Instead of using generic subheadings, though, use carefully chosen phrases that indicate what the next section is about.
- If the journals in your field don't use many subheadings, you may not be able to rely on them. That doesn't mean, however, that you can't use them while you're drafting. Think of them as temporary markers—cues to remind yourself to give special attention to transitions when you revise.

- If subheadings aren't practical, consider using extra white space to indicate that you've finished with one topic and are about to take up another.

- Once you're fairly happy with the overall structure of your piece, go back and see if you can write a forecasting statement that lets your reader know where you are headed. There's no need to be heavy handed about it, especially in a short paper or one that is fairly easy to follow. But when your piece is a long one and your argument is subtle or complicated, your readers will appreciate all the help you can give.

- Also at a later stage read through your draft, looking for ways you can use transitional phrases and echo links to indicate the relationship of ideas at the sentence level.

Scenario 2: Paying Attention to Genre Expectations

Although Booth doesn't mention it in his essay, another important rhetorical consideration is the genre the writer is working in. Just as creative writers choose to write in certain forms—the short story, the novel, the lyric poem, the drama—so do academic writers. Although the range of genres is wide and varies somewhat across disciplines, a list of the most common academic genres might include scholarly books, edited volumes, chapters contributed to an edited collection, journal articles, book reviews, essays, textbooks, grant proposals—even syllabi and course materials.

In our faculty writing groups I often begin by suggesting that everyone bring to the first meeting a copy of the journal in which they want to publish, a book by the publisher they are hoping to interest, or an RFP (request for proposals) for the grant they are starting to write. As we pass these around the group, one thing we always notice is how different our disciplines are in their expectations—something we need to keep in mind as we continue to work together as a group.

As the year goes on, however, we discover that even within our disciplines there are huge variations in what reviewers are looking for, what publishers expect, or what different funding agencies find persuasive. Often we advise each other to pay closer attention to the stated or implicit "rules" one is expected to follow to publish successfully in a particular place. Other times we urge each other to press against those constraints a little, to treat them as we hope our best students will treat the assignments we give them, that is, not as outlines to follow slavishly but as templates to use or depart from as the situation demands.

To some extent the decision of what genre to work in is determined by the conventions of the writer's field. A biologist doing research on insect genetics is expected to publish her results in a scientific journal. A legal scholar publishes in a law review. In some fields one cannot expect to get tenure without publishing a book; in others, new knowledge is produced so rapidly that conference papers and electronic journals are the primary outlets.

In many instances the genre is predetermined by the situation. An invitation to submit a chapter for an edited book is usually accompanied by guidelines on length, format, and other matters. An opportunity to speak in favor of a proposed policy change requires the writer to produce a well-supported argument.

In many instances, however, the writer has some choices or decisions to make about genre. Choosing to write for an audience of practitioners rather than an audience of scholars means that you may need to abandon the form of the research article in favor of a more informal essay. And deciding whether to turn a dissertation into a journal article or a book depends as much on your own time commitments as on the scope and complexity of the project.

In graduate school most of us get some preparation in how to write for the most common genres of our disciplines. However, once out of school we may have to learn new genres, and sometimes the learning is surprisingly difficult.

Julia, a long-time member of our group, has already established herself as a successful academic writer. With several published articles and a book to her credit, she feels fairly confident about her writing, but she enjoys the collegiality in the group and feels she always gets good ideas and suggestions when she brings a draft for us to read.

This year Julia has decided to apply for a prestigious program development grant from a well-known private foundation. It's a great opportunity to implement a university-community partnership she believes in and to fund the full-time support staff that will make the project work.

Although she has never written a major grant proposal before, Julia feels confident that she can make the case for the work she wants to do. What she sends out to the group is, in her view, a "nearly completed draft." While she is compiling the various appendixes and supporting documents to accompany the proposal, she would like us to make suggestions for how she can "polish the prose."

When we meet to discuss the draft, the first responses are all quite positive. Everyone likes the program Julia has envisioned, and we especially appreciate her clear, smooth writing style. One member of our group praises the introduction, which he says "really draws the reader in"; another comments positively on a striking analogy Julia has made.

Before long, though, it becomes apparent that not everyone feels the same way about the proposal. The scientists in the group are especially skeptical, having written and read enough proposals of their own to have a sense of what grant reviewers are looking for. "I'm not sure I understand what problem you're trying to address," one of them says. "And how will you be able to show that your program has accomplished what you want it to?"

Another experienced grant writer seconds that opinion. "I think you should get to the point more quickly; establish the need for this program. Don't forget that the people reading this proposal may be reviewing a stack of fifty to one hundred, all at the same time. They can't fund everything, so they're looking for reasons to eliminate anything they can. If they can't pick up your proposal and immediately see its significance, you're in trouble."

From her reaction to the scientists' comments, we can tell that this is not what Julia expected to hear. Most readers respond positively to her narrative writing style, so she is inclined to see the scientists' comments as rooted in disciplinary differences. However, she also respects the grant-writing experience they bring to the group.

When she asks for more explicit advice, one of the scientists is happy to provide it: "Just cut to the chase," he says. "You can probably compress that three-page introduction into one short, direct paragraph. Then outline the major problem you're addressing and explain how each aspect of your program will solve the problem."

At the mention of "solving the problem" Julia immediately interrupts. "That's not what this program is about," she says. "The problems I'm addressing are far too complex to be 'solved' so easily. That's the whole point I was making in that introduction. I don't want to make unreasonable claims for the program I'm proposing." She decides to leave the proposal the way it is.

One day during the next semester, Julia comes to our writing group with a sheepish expression on her face. She has just gotten the reviewers' comments from the grant proposal she sent in, and they are not at all what she had hoped for. However, some of those comments have a familiar ring.

"They say I haven't defined the problem clearly enough," says Julia, looking directly at the scientists. "And they want me to be more specific about how the program will meet the needs of the community. I guess I should have taken your advice in the first place."

When shifting from one academic genre to another, it often takes a while to learn the new rules. If we've had success in a different genre, this can be particularly frustrating because past success can lull us into thinking we have learned all we need to know about writing. This is often the case with new faculty members who have labored months or years to complete a dissertation, only to have to turn around, in their first year on the job, and convert that dissertation into a book or article that can be read by nonspecialists in the field.

In fact, learning the rules of a new genre isn't all that difficult. It just requires a willingness to track down models to emulate and a certain amount of flexibility to adapt to unfamiliar conventions. Once learned, the new conventions become part of the writer's repertoire—a collection of options and strategies that can be drawn from in future writing situations.

Getting Feedback from Others

If you're working in an unfamiliar genre, it's good to seek advice from people who have experience with that genre.

- Ask a few colleagues if they would share examples with you. This is particularly important if you're writing a proposal; those aren't published and are sometimes hard to come by. Be sure to ask for *successful* examples—grant proposals that were funded, conference proposals that were selected, book proposals that elicited expressions of interest. And make sure you get a variety to peruse. But unsuccessful proposals can be useful, too, especially if your colleagues are willing to share the reviewer comments.
- Make connections with people who regularly review manuscripts or proposals in that genre. On my campus we offer occasional proposal-writing workshops and invite faculty who serve as reviewers for funding agencies to talk about what they look for in the proposals they read. Their perspectives are always enlightening, which reminds us that even in these formal application processes, we need to understand and write for a specific audience.
- Another source of early feedback is the publisher or granting agency. Professional and textbook publishers use their Web sites to

share proposal guidelines and offer advice to potential authors. Many funding agencies do this as well. Most have program directors who can answer questions in advance, and some encourage proposal writers to send in "pre-proposals" that they will comment on. Journal editors tend to rely on published guidelines and the examples that appear in their pages to coach writers on what is expected, but some may respond to queries from writers as well.

One advantage of a writing group is that it broadens the range of experience you can draw on as you venture into new kinds of writing. This is especially true with a multidisciplinary group, but it's also the case with colleagues in the same discipline. We all read different journals, do different kinds of research, and gravitate toward different genres of academic writing. Thus we can offer our colleagues the benefit of our own experience as writers and readers in a variety of contexts.

Writing on Your Own

In addition to the help you can get from others, you may find "surrogate colleagues" on your own bookshelves or at your library, campus bookstore, or grants office.

• If you are totally unfamiliar with a certain genre, it's important to look for models early and seek out more than one; that way you can get a range of what is generally accepted.

• If you have a fairly good idea of what you are expected to do, go ahead and start writing. When unanticipated questions arise as you go ("Is it acceptable to write this in first person?" "Can I put the whole methodology section in an appendix?"), make a note and seek out examples to get a clearer sense of how much freedom you have within the genre.

• In some cases you may find books or writing guides especially helpful. When I co-taught a graduate course, "Writing in the Life Sciences," my teaching partner recommended a very useful book by

Robert Day titled *How to Write and Publish a Scientific Paper*. For me, a novice in the area of scientific writing, the book made explicit many of the implicit "rules" of the genre. Chances are you will find others in your own disciplines.

Scenario 3: Making Sense of the Conventions

Even when writers are familiar with an academic genre, they may have trouble if they don't think about *why* the genre works as it does. An abstract, for instance, performs an important function in a scientific paper. It allows other researchers to scan quickly through the latest issues of professional journals, finding studies that pertain to their own work. Because it is a capsule version of the whole paper, an abstract may use exact sentences that appear in the introduction or results section. Understanding that, the writer need not waste time looking for other (and perhaps less precise) ways of saying the same thing.

Although genre conventions can sometimes be puzzling, it is useful to think of them as templates that writers can follow or adapt to their own purposes. In the writing of this book I had difficulty at first understanding the difference between a preface and a first chapter that serves as introduction. Because I am often interested in hearing the story behind the book I am reading—how the writer became interested in the topic, how the book evolved along the way—I tend to blur the lines that my editor sees as more solid. After she explained that most of the material I had originally planned to include in my first chapter was more appropriate for the preface of a Jossey-Bass book, I wrote an extensive revision of those opening sections. Although I still might prefer to blur the distinction between preface and introduction, I chose to trust my editor's sense of what academic and professional readers expect when they pick up a book.

Conventions, like social manners, always evolve for a purpose. Once in place, though, they can sometimes calcify and feel more like meaningless rules than useful templates. If we follow these so-called rules without thinking about them, we risk making our writing dull and mechanical. If we understand and use conventions wisely, however, we generally find that they help us communicate effectively.

Claire, a respected practitioner with a wealth of practical experience to her credit, has taught for the past four years as a part-time clinical instructor in her field. This year for the first time she has been hired for a full-time position, which may be converted to tenure-track in the future. Last year Claire gave presentations at two professional conferences on a new procedure she has developed for practitioners in her field. Response from the audience was positive, and another panel member who reviews for one of the field's most respected journals suggested that she write up her work to submit for publication.

Although she is not required to publish to keep her position, Claire knows that a publication like this would be good for her career. It would set her up for a tenure-track position, should one become available, and would ensure that she gets credit for the work she has done. When she brings the piece to our writing group, she asks us to pay special attention to its scholarly format. Unlike the writing she has been doing on the job, this piece has to follow the form of a scientific paper, and Claire feels a little rusty in this area.

We begin, as usual, by having everyone say something positive about the piece of writing. When two people comment on the "thoroughness" of her literature review section, Claire is clearly pleased. The section was boring to write, she says, and she feared that it was too long and boring to read. She had no idea what to include and what to leave out, so she just made sure to mention every article she could find in her disciplinary database that related somehow to her subject.

At this, another member of our group nods her head. "I know what you mean," she says. "I had a hard time getting through this section. But I don't think it's just a question of length. What are you trying to do in this lit review? Are you providing important information to your readers or just establishing your credibility as a researcher?"

At first Claire doesn't know how to respond to the question. In grad school, where she learned how to write scientific papers, no one had ever talked about the purpose of the lit review. It just had to be there, after the introduction and before the methodology section. After a couple of minutes of fumbling around for an answer, she says that she's doing both these things: providing information about the kinds of procedures available but also establishing herself as an expert in the field. And she is also leading up to talking about the procedure she has developed. "Everyone knows," she says, "that the most commonly used procedures have a lot of weaknesses. It's just that the better ones are too costly to use on a regular basis. What I've done is to take one of the more costly procedures and redesign it so that it can be used simply and cost-effectively."

"I think you've just answered your own question," someone says. (It's amazing how often we have these "aha!" moments.) "All you need to do is write it the way you just explained it to us: 'The most commonly used procedures are A, B, and C, but each has serious flaws, and so on. A far better choice is the D procedure, because it does such and such. In this paper I will outline a modified D procedure, which I call E. It has the advantage of being both accurate and cost-effective and can be used by everyone.' Each time you mention a different procedure, you credit the person who developed it. When you mention the flaws, you cite whoever pointed them out. Later, when you're explaining your own idea, you can refer back to the sources you've cited and mention others if you need to at that point."

At first Claire is skeptical. The suggested revision will cut the literature review section in half. But when she sees how much we all like our colleague's suggestion, she starts to see its worth as well.

"I never realized that the lit review could actually help me make my point," she says.

Is it always this easy? Of course not. But understanding the conventions always makes it easier to use them to advantage. In this case the terminology itself may contribute to that lack of understanding.

The term *literature review* suggests that the purpose of this section of an academic paper or book should be to review the professional literature that relates to the book or article's subject. In most cases, however, this is not at all what is needed. Instead, what the lit review *should* do is to sketch out for the reader the intellectual path that the writer has followed in order that readers may follow it as well.

This is what our colleague did when he outlined Claire's lit review for her—or rather, when he sketched out the outline he heard implicit in what she told us. The significant point about this newly imagined outline is that it allows Claire's readers to see into her thinking, preparing them to be convinced by the evidence she will present.

Another thing that complicates the writing of a good literature review is the fact that many of us bring from graduate school the bad habit of writing for teachers or dissertation directors who expect "proper format" without encouraging us to think about the purposes that lie behind academic conventions. In the case of lit reviews in particular, we are often so intent on showing that we've read everything we were supposed to read—something that dissertation directors often expect—that we don't even think about the reasons for including a literature review in a professional article.

A while back I wrote an essay about this subject that appeared on the back page of the *Chronicle of Higher Education* (Rankin, 1998). In the essay, I cited several examples of problematic literature reviews, speculated about why they are so prevalent, and explained the legitimate functions that a good literature review can serve, among them, establishing the writer's credibility, meeting the readers' needs, and clarifying the theoretical framework of the work at hand.

Immediately I heard from people all over the country who shared my sense that the academic literature review is one of the deadliest features of academic writing. The notion that it doesn't have to be was something most of them had not considered.

Getting Feedback from Others

If you're working in an unfamiliar genre, it's always good to seek writing advice from others who regularly write in that genre. They can tell you what the conventions are and give you good practical pointers. But just as important as knowing the conventions is knowing why they have evolved as they have. So when you're seeking advice, seek out writers who are thoughtful about the reasons behind the conventions. Ask them to explain why the conventions work as they do. If they can give you answers (not everyone can), you'll be better equipped to work within the conventions and better able to make good decisions about how far you can stretch them.

Writing on Your Own

If you don't have a writing group, you can still teach yourself to develop the habit of questioning genre conventions. One of the best ways to do this is to become more conscious of how those conventions affect you as a reader.

- As you read published work in your field, think about the genre conventions that underlie that work. Are those conventions fairly firm and explicit? Are they actually taught in graduate school and explained in professional manuals? Or are they more flexible and implicit, learned primarily by consciously or unconsciously imitating the way others write?
- When you find yourself reading an academic or professional book or article that you find particularly engaging, stop and think about how the piece is structured. Does it follow the expected conventions of your field? If not, is this a problem or a refreshing change?
- Likewise, tune in to what you notice when reading a book or article that you find dull, mechanical, or confusing. Is the writer following conventions too slavishly? What changes might have made the piece more readable?

Scenario 4: Dealing with Difficult Situations

Much of the writing we do in academic and professional contexts is directed at people like ourselves: academically trained scholars and professional colleagues who have grown accustomed to working their way through dense and difficult texts. But that's not always the case. In our faculty writing groups, for instance, we have read each other's newsletter articles, practitioner guides, personal essays, textbooks, syllabi, and letters of recommendation for students. Often when people bring in such a piece, they apologize, as if it were not "real writing," not serious enough or important enough to warrant the attention of the group. Yet these nonscholarly pieces frequently prove to be as challenging for the writer as any scientific paper or scholarly analytic essay. And at the heart of the problem, more often than not, is some uncertainty about purpose and audience.

Walt doesn't often bring work to the writing group. He's a regular participant and always has pertinent things to say about others' writing, but his own research area is so technical that he knows we probably wouldn't understand it. One semester, though, he says he has a project that we can help him with. His department has just finished a major curriculum overhaul, and he's been asked to write up the new program option for majors. It's a short piece, he says, so he'll just bring it with him when he comes to our meeting.

The day we're scheduled to talk about the piece, Walt stops by my office to say he'll be a little late for our meeting. He leaves copies of the piece with me, suggesting that we go ahead and read it and he'll get there as soon as he can. After Walt leaves my office, I realize he hasn't provided the cover sheet we always ask for, telling us what we need to know to understand what we're reading. If we have questions, we'll just have to wait and ask Walt when he arrives.

And we do have questions. As soon as we begin reading the three-page draft, brows begin to furrow and puzzled muttering can be heard. "I thought he said we would understand this!" someone says, and the rest of us laugh and shake our heads. The material certainly isn't technical, but we're all having trouble understanding the program explanation. How many options are there now for majors in the field—two or three? And if there are three, what is the difference between the second and third?

By the time Walt arrives, we have gotten a little giddy in our confusion. Nick is at the blackboard, trying to outline the three program options he thinks he sees, and the rest of us are calling out conflicting interpretations of Walt's explanation.

Walt himself is clearly chagrined. He had hoped this would be a short and simple writing task, but he sees now that it won't be. When someone asks who will be reading this description, he says it's just a news release he's been asked to write.

A news release? We were assuming it was more like catalog copy, that is, information provided for potential and current students, high school counselors, academic advisers, or professional accrediting agencies. Well, that's true, Walt says. But there's another issue here as well.

The new option, it turns out, is designed to attract more majors in a department that is worried about its numbers dropping steadily over the past few years. Already there are two options in the department: one for potential research scholars who will go on to graduate school and the other for those who want to teach at the secondary level. This new major is designed to attract a third group of students: those interested in combining an interest in research and business and preparing for management positions.

For Walt and his colleagues the plan makes practical sense, but they have mixed feelings about it. Because they are research scholars themselves, they believe strongly in the traditional major and see the new option, which has fewer specific requirements, as a "watered-down" version of the major. When he explains it this way, we see another source of the confusion. Not only is Walt unsure what he's writing here (catalog copy or recruiting brochure) but his own deep ambivalence about the new program is leaking through in the language he's using.

For instance, in one place Walt describes the new program as being "of interest to students who want to avoid advanced prerequisite courses." That language itself is a clue to Walt's big rhetorical problem: how to get the word out to students who might be attracted to the new major option without suggesting that those students probably just aren't smart enough to succeed in the standard program.

We finally suggest that Walt throw out this draft and start over, but not before he has consulted with his department about the purpose and intended audience of the document he has been asked to write. If the task is to provide clear catalog copy, then neutral language, brief explanations, and a list of requirements for each program should be sufficient. But if the idea is to attract more students, both content and tone may need to be more overtly persuasive.

As this example illustrates, an overfocus on content at the expense of purpose and audience isn't the exclusive domain of scholarly essays. It can show up in other kinds of writing as well. Think of all the reports, memos, and proposals that have crossed your desk in the past month. How many of them could have been improved had the writer given more thought to who would be reading them and for what purpose?

Getting Feedback from Others

When you have conflicted feelings about the subject you are writing on, your ambivalence may, like Walt's, color your writing in ways you are unaware of. Writing groups are good at picking up on these attitudes, even when you think you've managed to keep them hidden. By drawing you out and getting you to articulate your feelings about the subject, colleagues can help you untangle complicated issues and face difficult rhetorical problems head on. They may also be able to help you better understand your audience's point of view, so you don't inadvertently alienate the very people you're trying to reach.

- If you have the opportunity, it is always good to test your writing with the audience it is intended for. Students are often flattered to be asked to read early drafts of their professor's textbook-in-progress, and practitioners are rarely shy about critiquing writing that is aimed at them. When you give them your work, tell them you need their honest reactions. Because they represent the audience you want to reach, their feedback will be especially valuable to you.

- If you don't have access to readers who represent your intended audience, ask a colleague, friend, or your writing group to role play that audience. In the scenario just described, it was easy for us to imagine ourselves as students, but that's not always the case. Sometimes you may need to coach your readers on how they should play their roles. Explain what your audience will be looking for. What will they already know about the subject? What will be new or controversial? Your readers may not be able to assume the role completely, but they can do well enough to give you some useful feedback.

Writing on Your Own

Reading through the eyes of the intended audience is one of the hardest things a writer has to do, and it is always a poor substitute for having real readers available to assume the audience's perspective. Still, every writer is capable of developing an "other self" who can play the critical role of audience at various points during the writing process.

- The key is to get in the habit of thinking about audience early in the planning process. Who will be reading this piece and for what purpose? If you find you can't answer the question, it may mean you're not ready to begin. Don't interpret this question too narrowly, though. Few of us know *exactly* who we are writing for, and if we think about it too long, we can convince ourselves that no one will ever read what we write.

- Once you have written a draft, the challenge is to read it through the eyes of the intended audience. Don't even try to do this, however, until you have let it sit for a while. It may take some time and critical distance to get inside your readers' skin, especially if you're a little thin-skinned yourself, as so many of us are about our writing.

Scenario 5: Resisting the Temptation to Recycle

Writers who do a lot of work in the same subject area often find themselves tempted to recycle material written for one project by using it in another. Although this certainly works in some instances, it can create problems if the writer is not attuned to the differences between the original rhetorical situation and the new one.

In his first year as a faculty member, Nathan has been encouraged by his department to begin applying for research grants immediately. When he brings us the introduction to the proposal he is working on, he explains that it is for a prestigious grant that focuses on both research and teaching. The research component he is fairly confident about because it is an extension of his dissertation work. The teaching component is less well developed, but he knows it will involve undergraduate research opportunities.

When we meet to talk about Nathan's draft, we spend a lot of time at first asking questions about the granting agency. What are they looking for? What kinds of research do they support? In the course of answering our questions, Nathan explains that he doesn't expect to get funded on the first try. It rarely works that way. But he hopes to get reviewer comments that will help him revise and resubmit. Right now he just wants to know if this introduction makes sense.

For us that's not an easy question to answer. The chapter does make sense on a certain level: as a general introduction to Nathan's research topic. But we are not sure it makes sense as a proposal. For one thing it's hard to distinguish what Nathan has already done in the course of his dissertation research from what he plans to do with new funding from this agency. For another there is nothing in the introduction about how or why Nathan plans to involve students in his research.

The more we press Nathan for answers to our questions, the more he falls back on what he said in the beginning: "It's OK if it's not perfect now because I'll have to resubmit anyway. I just want to get it out there and get some comments."

"OK," someone says, "but why send out a really early draft when you could send something further along?"

"Oh, it's not an early draft," Nathan replies. "Most of this comes directly from my dissertation, and that went through several revisions!"

Eventually we let the matter drop, sensing that Nathan is getting frustrated with our questions. But when he comes back the next week, we realize that he has heard us after all.

"You were right about that grant proposal," he says. "I asked my partner to read it, and she said the same thing. I guess I was trying to save time by using what I had already written."

This happens often in our writing groups. We make a suggestion the writer resists at the time but then accedes to later for one reason or another. In this case Nathan had time to reflect on our advice and to ask someone else, who confirmed it. What he had written with one purpose and audience in mind didn't transfer easily to the other, despite the fact that there was considerable overlap between the two projects. Although he thought he could save time by using the earlier material, this turned out to be a false economy on his part, a move that would probably cost him more time and revision effort in the long run.

This is not to say that Nathan couldn't use any of the earlier dissertation material. In fact, he eventually did. But to do that he had to resist the temptation to *start* with that material; instead, he needed to step back and outline a coherent new proposal that provided the necessary background information, defined a clear research question, described a workable methodology, and included a meaningful teaching component. Once he had that in place, he found that he could indeed use bits and pieces from his dissertation, especially in the background section of his proposal.

Now here is an interesting side note. At one point while working on an earlier version of this chapter, I considered including, in its complete form, the *Chronicle of Higher Education* essay I mentioned in a previous section. At the time I was convinced that it said everything I wanted to say about the problematic convention of the lit review, and it had the virtue of being already written. When I mentioned the idea to my editor, she was remarkably gentle with her response: "I like the way you have dealt with the lit review theme in the *Chronicle* article," she wrote, "but I am less keen on just plunking this opinion piece into your chapter as you propose. I'd rather see an adapted version meshed into the new chapter content."

She was right of course. And the fact that I had even considered the idea is further evidence of how strong the temptation to recycle can be.

Getting Feedback from Others

If you use some older material in a new draft, your own desire to make it work may cloud your judgment. That's why it's good to ask a colleague or writing group to read your draft. Here are two ways you might do this:

• To see if the old material fits in smoothly with the new, don't tell your readers what you've done. Just ask them to tell you if the piece reads smoothly and coherently. If they comment on spots where the old material was inserted, you'll know the seams are showing.

- If you would rather focus readers' attention on this particular issue, explain that you've used some previously written material and ask them to keep an eye out for it. If they can spot it with just that general cue, it's probably not blended in smoothly.

Writing on Your Own

If you're working alone, you may have to take preventive measures to keep yourself from giving in to temptation.

- If you're starting work on a new project that overlaps with something you have done before, resist the temptation to open up the old material and try to work from that. Instead, outline a structure and draft an opening for the new piece, making sure it is appropriate to the present rhetorical situation, that is, the purpose and audience you are writing for now.

- Write all the way through the draft, leaving blank spots wherever you think you can use the older material. When you've finished a complete draft, come back and see if the old material fits in. If it does, use it, being sure to smooth the transitions between old and new.

As Wayne Booth reminds us, writing is first and foremost a job to be done for a particular audience. To write effectively in academic and professional contexts, we must learn to think rhetorically, that is, to balance the demands of the subject against our own intents and purposes and the needs and expectations of readers.

4

Finding Your Professional Voice

In the round of positive comments that always precedes any critiques or suggestions we offer in our writing groups, one comment that comes up over and over is, "I can really hear your voice here." In the early days the comment often came from me. When others said something similar, they might allude to "sounding like Libby," and I began to wonder whether the "voice thing" was just my personal campaign. After a while, though, I noticed that comments about voice were coming from all quarters. Even the scientists, who generally believed that there was no room for voice in their writing, were appreciative of the historian's irrepressible enthusiasm for his subject. And we all looked forward to the days when our counseling psychology colleague would bring in her work, replete with humorous anecdotes and ironic commentary.

But what is it we mean when we talk about the voice in a piece of writing? According to Peter Elbow, we may be referring to several different but related metaphorical concepts, one of which he calls "resonance" or "presence"—the quality that allows us to "sense the fit between the voice in a text and the unknown writer behind it" (Elbow, 2000, p. 211). This is probably what most of us mean when we use that word. When we notice voice in a piece of writing, it is a human presence we are picking up on, a sense of someone connecting with us on a personal level. It need not be an intimate level. If you have ever read a speech by Martin Luther King Jr., you know

that some people can connect in that way with huge crowds of people. And it's certainly possible to do it in scholarly books, professional
papers, or even grant applications, as we know from encountering
those all-too-rare examples in our scholarly and professional reading.

For many of us the notion of finding a comfortable and resonant
professional voice is attractive yet challenging. We hate sounding
stuffy, mechanical, and dull. But we also worry about sacrificing traditional academic values such as professional distance and objectivity. Although finding a voice may entail having the courage to
challenge the more conservative conventions of academic writing—
conventions that encourage passive verbs and forbid first-person
pronouns, for instance—it need not be as difficult as it seems. Finding a voice is mostly a matter of developing an ear for language and
having the confidence to integrate who you are as a person with
who you are as a professional.

Scenario 1: Claiming Ownership of Your Writing

In some cases we associate voice with the personal pronoun, that
is, the "I" or "we" a writer uses in a sentence like this one. But matters of voice are far more subtle and complex than that. In our writing group, for instance, the historian didn't use a single first-person
pronoun. Still, his voice came through in his sentence rhythms and
in the lively, colorful language he used in writing animatedly about
his favorite subject.

Most of us probably aren't aware of choosing a voice to write in.
We just write. And if what we read in our professional journals is
generally written in a formal, impersonal, slightly distant voice, we
learn to take on a similar voice when we enter the professional conversation.

This is not to say that there is anything inherently wrong with
writing in a voice that is formal, impersonal, and distant. In fact,
some situations demand it, and some writers handle it gracefully. The

problem comes when the formality impedes communication, when the impersonality obscures the presence of the human mind, when the distance separates the writer from her own words.

For Marie the process of finding her own professional voice has been a struggle from the beginning. As the daughter of two college professors, she literally grew up in an academic discourse community. Given that her own discipline is dominated by traditional male scientists, it is no surprise that when she sits down to write, what emerges on the page is that formal academic voice.

In the first piece Marie brings to our writing group—a piece she has been working on for some time—the scientific voice is firmly in control. Full of technical language, disciplinary jargon, and passive sentence constructions ("the data were analyzed"), the piece describes Marie's fieldwork methods and findings in carefully documented detail.

Although several of us in the writing group find the piece very slow going, those in other scientific and technical fields have less difficulty with it. Well socialized in the discourse of objective science, they have learned to read this densely packed prose as easily (well, almost as easily) as the rest of us read academic essays in our own fields. By the end of our session they have given Marie lots of good feedback, including several suggestions for clarifying and reorganizing her material, and Marie has taken careful notes so she won't forget anything they have said.

As we start to pack up our things, someone asks Marie how she feels about the feedback she got, and she sighs deeply. "It's OK," she says. "I just need to do it I guess."

"Just do it" is often good advice to give ourselves as writers, but in this case Marie doesn't sound resolved. It's not that she has lost interest in her research, she tells us. In fact the research is still a powerful attraction for her, and she can hardly wait to get back to her fieldwork site next summer. It's the *writing* she has lost all interest in. She doesn't know if she has the will to get it done.

When we press Marie to talk about her frustration, she tells us that in the field she feels totally involved in her work. Out there "on the ground" there is no separation between who she is as a scientist and who she is as a person: mother, teacher, gardener, movie lover, novel reader, lover of good food and exotic jewelry. When she starts to write, though, she immediately feels alienated from all that. She feels as if she's been told to check her colorful caftan at the door and walk into this academic cocktail party wearing plain brown prison garb. "I just hate this kind of writing," she says. "I can do it, but I hate it."

We can sympathize. After all, we've written dissertations. And many of us have succumbed to pressure to churn out papers we didn't feel like writing in voices that didn't seem like our own.

So we understand Marie's frustration and her desire to just get this thing over with. But we wonder if there might be something she can do in the meantime to overcome the alienation she is feeling and to claim ownership of her writing.

What if she just took a page—any page at random—and tried to rewrite it in a style she likes better? Might some of those passive verbs, for instance, be converted to active voice? And couldn't some of that opaque jargon be translated into perfectly acceptable layman's language? After all, Marie is writing about the *people* of an earlier age, and yet her prose seems to be burying the very human evidence her excavations have unearthed.

A week or two later, Marie arrives at our session with a single sheet of paper in hand. What she has written is one paragraph that she struggled nearly three hours to rewrite. But she can see the difference. We can see it, too, not only on the page but in Marie's face and in her body language. It will be a while yet before she finds her voice as a writer, but at least she has a sense of where to look for it.

Why should academic and professional writing be dull? Think about it. No matter what our discipline or area of research, we are drawn to it because we find it interesting and intellectually engaging (most of the time anyway). In conversation with lively colleagues, our voices communicate the commitment we feel to our subject, and when asked about our work, we become more animated, more at ease. People just entering the room are also drawn to our conversation group. They sense the passion and commitment we feel for our work.

If this happens in other professional contexts such as in labs, in coffee lounges, at conferences, and in graduate seminars, why can't it happen in the pages of our professional publications?

Getting Feedback from Others

One advantage of working with a writing group is that you get to read other people's writing, hear other people's stories, steal other people's problem-solving strategies. On the issue of voice, there is no better teacher than the writing of colleagues who have somehow broken through the welter of dull, lifeless prose and found a way to balance a professional demeanor with an engaging personal style. In fact, how they made the breakthrough is often as instructive as the example of their writing. In our group one writer who had been invited to submit an article for a special issue of a journal in his field simply didn't have time to revise a conference presentation before the editor's deadline. He sent the paper off in its existing form, fully expecting to be asked to do extensive revision. To his surprise the revisions the editor asked for were very minor ones, and none had to do with what our colleague saw as the informal style of the piece.

You can also use your group and supportive colleagues as test readers when you experiment with different voices.

- If you find it difficult to hear your own voice, have your readers help you listen for it. Ask them to mark any sentence or passage in your writing that sounds especially like you. Then study these passages to see what the common elements are.
- When trying out a new voice, bring a draft or just a piece of a draft to your group or a supportive colleague and ask them what they

think. If they don't think it works, they can tell you gently. If they like it, their encouragement may be all you need to keep trying.

• Get the group involved in the writing. Bring in a sample piece of prose that you find particularly deadly. It might be your own prose or something you've read. See if the group can rewrite it in a livelier style without losing any part of the meaning.

Seeing others succeed at finding their voice can be an inspiration for risk-averse academic writers. Sometimes the "rules" we think we must follow turn out to be figments of our imagination.

Writing on Your Own

If the prospect of finding your own voice as an academic or professional writer seems daunting, consider trying to do it in increments, just a little at a time.

• If you find it difficult to write in the formal voice required in many academic and professional contexts, write your first drafts in a more relaxed, informal voice. After you've succeeded in getting your ideas down on paper, you can come back and tighten up your style.

• Don't get hung up on pronouns. If you like to write in the first person, go ahead and use it in your first drafts. You can always convert it to third person later. If first person doesn't feel comfortable, don't use it. But do try to make your writing more like your speech, whatever that might mean. Don't worry that your voice may be too informal. It's much easier to polish a rough-hewn sentence than it is to lighten a stuffy one.

• If you want to enliven your style but don't know where to begin, buy a good style book that includes exercises (not just injunctions), and try practicing on your own. My favorite is Joseph Williams's *Style: Ten Lessons in Clarity and Grace* (1999). See Appendix C for further information.

• When you encounter an academic or professional writer whose voice you admire, copy a few sample pages and keep them on hand.

Reread them for inspiration when you begin a writing project of your own or when you feel you may be falling into a voice you don't like.

- If the constraints of your discipline or profession don't give you much room to find your own voice, look for opportunities to practice in situations that offer more flexibility. Many professional journals publish book reviews, opinion pieces, letters to the editor, and pedagogical essays that may be written in a more relaxed style than a scholarly article. Likewise, many professional organizations have newsletters or bulletins you might try writing for. And you can always try out your voice in local campus newsletters, departmental brochures, and self-produced course materials. The voice (or voices) you cultivate in these arenas might not immediately transfer to your more formal writing, but the confidence you gain when you integrate your personal and professional voices will be a boon to your writing in the long run.

Scenario 2: Exorcising the Grad Student Within

Although "resonant voice" or "presence" may make a piece of writing more credible, for many academic writers the issue of voice may have more to do with authority. On the surface, Peter Elbow says, this may seem to be a function of the writer's personality, that is, whether he or she has "the conviction or the self-trust or gumption to make her voice carry." But that isn't always the case. "It's not unusual, for example, for someone to develop a voice with strong authority that doesn't match their sense of who they are—or our sense of who they are" (p. 204). In other words, the voice of authority is one that we can learn to cultivate.

After helping to organize a successful conference on a new theoretical approach to work in her field, Lucy is asked to coedit a collection of papers coming out of the conference. Pleased that this will give her some national visibility and the opportunity to have a real impact on her profession, Lucy agrees to work on the project with a colleague on a distant campus. Because her coeditor will secure permissions and do most of the correspondence with contributors, Lucy agrees to draft the introductory chapter to the volume.

Although she has never written this kind of thing before, Lucy has looked at several edited collections to get a sense of what an introduction should look like. She knows she needs to set the theoretical context, explain how the volume came about, and briefly preview the various contributions. When she brings her draft to the group, she is primarily concerned about the tone of the introduction. These papers constitute a major shift in the direction her field has traditionally taken, but she cannot afford to alienate traditional scholars, who still train most graduate students and will have considerable influence on whether the volume is used in graduate courses or simply ignored by all but Lucy's fellow revolutionaries.

As we read the draft she has written, we see lots of evidence of Lucy's hyperconsciousness of audience. She begins by explaining how the new approach builds on work done by earlier scholars but departs from that work in significant ways. Although she is worried that her reference to the earlier scholars may not sound respectful enough, our concern is that it may be *too* respectful. In her determination not to offend her predecessors, she has made it sound as if the gaps they left unexplored are relatively minor ones. As she goes on to describe the new theoretical approach, she spends two full pages saying what the approach is *not:* not anti-empirical, not radically political, not interested in trivia at the expense of the big picture. When someone remarks that this sounds rather defensive, Lucy says she thinks it is necessary because the new approach is so often misrepresented in the existing literature. In fact, to make the case for its legitimacy she has devoted several paragraphs to explaining the intellectual history of the new theoretical perspective, quoting well-known scholars in other fields and citing dozens of articles that lay the theoretical groundwork.

Although we are impressed with the work Lucy has done on this project and with the breadth of learning she displays in this introduction, we find that it distracts us from the main point she is making. Her point is that previous scholars have left questions unanswered and that these are interesting and important questions requiring a new theoretical approach—an approach illustrated by the essays in this volume.

When we point this out, Lucy admits that she is not happy with the introduction. "I think I've lost touch with my own voice," she tells us. "I feel like I'm back in graduate school, trying to please my professors and show them how much I know."

"I know what you mean," says one of our colleagues. "We thought when we became professors that we were beyond those kinds of feelings. And yet every time we find ourselves challenging the accepted wisdom in our field, the graduate student inside us comes out and says, 'Hey, I know this stuff. I really do. And if you don't believe me, here are umpteen citations that will bear me out.'"

After further discussion we suggest that Lucy go back and rewrite the introduction. It's fine, we tell her, to link the essays in her collection with the work of previous scholars in her field. In fact, this is just what new scholars have to do to find their place in the professional conversation. But that doesn't mean she has to bow and scrape to do it.

Who is this "graduate student inside us" who keeps popping up at inauspicious times? It is the self-assured yet hesitant, assertive yet deferential and conflicted self that emerges whenever we find ourselves paying less attention to what we're saying than to how it will be received. For Wayne Booth this overawareness of audience usually results in a rhetorical imbalance that he calls the "advertiser's stance" (p. 143). In academic and professional writing, though, it might be more appropriately thought of as the "dissertation stance." Cautious, risk-averse, and ever attuned to status in the established hierarchy, the dissertation stance is responsible for much of the writing we encounter in academic and professional discourse. It helps explain the overuse of citations and qualifiers, as well as the frequent calls for "further research."

Although some academic and professional writers adopt the dissertation stance in virtually everything they write, most of us probably revert to it only when we are feeling particularly vulnerable as writers. We do it, for example, when we deal with a new topic, address an unfamiliar audience, or challenge a generally accepted idea. In these situations we may sometimes *feel* like graduate students again, but if we are to persuade others to accept our ideas, we need to speak in the voice of the confident professional.

Getting Feedback from Others

If you suspect that the grad student within may be infiltrating your writing, mention it to the colleagues you have asked to read your work. They may be able to help in a number of ways.

- If the style of your prose feels too tentative, ask your readers to help you edit it. Have them cross out unnecessary qualifiers like "possibly" and change weak verbs like "might" and "would" to the stronger "will." In some cases you may choose to retain some of the language you originally used, but at that point you will be using it consciously, not just because you were writing in a tentative "graduate student voice."

- If your own voice tends to get lost among the citations, ask your readers to help you edit a page or two where this is happening. Chances are they will see better than you can which citations are really necessary and useful and which seem to be there just for show.

Writing on Your Own

Although it is possible to deal with these problems in the editing stage, as Lucy did, it is easier and more efficient to keep them from occurring in the first place.

- When you begin a piece of writing, think about the voice you want to project. Try to visualize yourself speaking at a professional conference and getting an enthusiastic reception from your peers. What did your voice sound like in that presentation? Can you make the same thing happen on the page?

- If you cannot visualize yourself in such a circumstance, take on the persona of a scholar, writer, or colleague you admire. Or imagine a whole alter ego—a secret self you summon up to do your writing for you and then tuck away in your office drawer until the next time she's needed.

- If certain readers in your potential audience intimidate you, try using the trick that public speakers use: imagine them reading in their underwear. Or better yet imagine them as they might have been as your seventh grade classmates. If you can get them off the pedestal they occupy in your mind, you can more easily address them as peers.

- If you're writing about something related to your thesis or dissertation, resist the temptation to use parts of that work in the piece you're writing now. It may pull you back into a graduate student persona without your even realizing it.

Scenario 3: Making It Personal

Closely related to the concept of voice is the issue of "the personal" in academic writing. For many of us, there is a strong connection between our personal lives and our scholarly work. Isn't it legitimate, even desirable, to acknowledge that personal investment? There are issues of intellectual honesty here, as well as concerns about professional objectivity. In our faculty groups we have lively discussions about matters like these, with some of us urging colleagues to "include a personal example" and others advising to "take out the personal stuff." Of course, disciplinary conventions have a lot to do with this. In some fields there is little room for personal anecdotes or reflections of any kind. In others there is a wider range of differences in style—from publisher to publisher, journal to journal, even editor to editor. Although some editors are adamant in their belief that the personal has no place in academic or professional writing, others see it as an appropriate acknowledgment of the personal agendas that always influence our professional work. For them the only concern may be how well you handle the material.

Unlike many of us Christine seems to have no problem integrating her personal and scholarly selves. A committed feminist who firmly believes that "the personal is political," Christine draws frequently on her own experiences to illustrate the gender differences she investigates in her scholarly work, and her lively voice and humor permeate her writing.

Last month when she was giving a presentation at a national conference, Christine was approached by an editor for a well-known academic publisher who suggested she write a book on the topic of her talk. Flattered by the editor's attention and excited by the positive response to her presentation, Christine agreed to put a proposal together and get it to the editor by the end of the month.

When she announces this to the writing group, Christine is already hard at work on the proposal. She has been in e-mail correspondence with the editor, who tells her to write in the same lively voice she used in her conference presentation, and the editor's faith in her work spurs Christine to get the proposal in on deadline.

Given all the encouragement she has gotten, Christine is taken aback two months later when the reviews come back sounding surprisingly negative. Although all three reviewers find things to like in the proposal, they say it sounds more like a popular self-help book than a serious academic treatment of the subject. Christine needs to establish more theoretical groundwork, they say, and refer more often to the work of established researchers. Finally, the whole book simply needs to be more "scholarly" in tone.

The reviews themselves are disappointing, but her editor's response to them is especially discouraging. Although she has tried to mitigate the criticism by telling Christine to ignore the most negative reviewer's remarks, the editor seems to like the other reviewers' suggestions and advises Christine to revise in third person and aim for a more formal academic tone.

It is this last suggestion that Christine resists most strongly. That "formal academic tone" is just what she prides herself on having expunged from her post-dissertation writing. She's not about to go back to it now, just to please readers who get nervous when they see a first-person pronoun! Besides, wasn't it this editor who had been encouraging her to write in her natural voice?

When Christine reads the reviewers' and editor's comments to the writing group, she isn't looking for advice so much as letting off steam. At this point she's not sure what to do, but she's already lost her enthusiasm for the project. Maybe she'll just set the piece aside for a while and work on something else.

Two months pass before Christine can get back to the project; when she does, she finds the revising difficult. As her writing group date approaches, she announces that she hasn't finished as much as she would have liked to. Could she just bring a few pages and read them aloud to us? If we like them, she'll continue writing. If not . . . .

Because we don't want Christine to give up on her book, we all want to like the new version. But as we listen, our responses are split. Some of us like it, but others think it has lost all its character. Christine herself is in the latter group. She knows she can do what the editor asked, but if the proposal gets good reviews this time, she'll have to write the whole book in this "scholarly" voice. She's not sure she wants to do that.

At this point someone asks a question no one had thought to ask before: Is Christine sure she has to do everything the editor suggested? She can beef up the theoretical section and add references to the other researchers—no problem. But what if, instead of eliminating all the first-person references, she just toned them down a bit?

For instance, she can use the same examples without indicating that they are from her own experience. And she can probably get rid of a few of the I's without doing much damage to the voice.

Although she is clearly skeptical, Christine is willing to give this strategy a try. If the editor doesn't like it, she can always revise yet again.

But the editor does like it. In an e-mail Christine forwards to us, she writes: "Good work on the revision! I think this addresses the reviewers' concerns. In fact, I'm not even going to send it back to them. Let's get to work!"

Because the scholarly ideal of objectivity (elusive as it may be) is so pervasive in academic and professional culture, the writer who chooses to use first-person pronouns and personal anecdotes may meet a fair bit of resistance. Still, writers who question the validity of the personal-professional boundary are making inroads in some areas. Even the *Publication Manual of the American Psychological Association*, one of the most conservative arbiters of academic correctness, now encourages researchers to refer to themselves in the first person (1994, p. 29). And reasonable editors like the one Christine was working with are often ready to make allowances for judicious use of "the personal."

What constitutes judicious use? There are no firm guidelines on that. Much depends, of course, on the subject matter and on the style conventions of the discipline. In my own field it is not at all unusual to encounter personal examples in academic writing. In scientific and technical disciplines, however, the personal is often discouraged.

Regardless of discipline it is generally best to keep personal anecdotes short and not *too* personal and to use first-person pronouns sparingly; this keeps the focus on the subject rather than the writer. To illustrate, here are a couple of passages that appeared in early drafts of this book, along with the revision that I made later:

Original: In some cases, you may find books or writing guides especially helpful. When I co-taught a graduate course in Writing in the Life Sciences, my teaching partner recommended a very useful book by Robert Day called *How to Write and Publish a Scientific Paper.* For me, a novice in the area of scientific writing, the book made explicit many of the implicit "rules" of the genre. Since then, colleagues have pointed me toward a number of books that offer advice in other fields and genres of writing. Since I'm not an expert in all those fields, I won't presume to make recommendations. (Besides, I know that what one reader sees as helpful advice, another may regard as useless.) What I do suggest is that you keep an eye out for helpful books on writing in your discipline. (And if they're books I should know about, please let me know!)

Revised: In some cases, you may find books or writing guides especially helpful. When I co-taught a graduate course in Writing in the Life Sciences, my teaching partner recommended a very useful book by Robert Day called *How to Write and Publish a Scientific Paper.* For me, a novice in the area of scientific writing, the book made explicit many of the implicit "rules" of the genre. Chances are, you will find others in your own disciplines. [Reduced from ten I-me-my pronouns to three!]

Original: In faculty discussions of writing on our campus, one topic that comes up way too often, in my view, is APA style.

Revised: Although conventions, like social manners, always evolve for a purpose, once in place they can sometimes calcify and feel more like meaningless rules than useful templates. If we follow these "rules" without thinking about them, we risk making our writing dull and mechanical. If we understand and use conventions wisely, however, we generally find that they help us communicate effectively. [Here the revision went well beyond wording. In the first draft I was venting my own frustration with instructors who focus on the format of their students' papers at the expense of larger rhetorical and content issues. In the second I focused on the real issue: the importance of understanding the rhetorical basis of genre conventions.]

Because I use first-person voice and examples throughout this book, these changes may not seem as dramatic as if I had eliminated the personal altogether. In these particular instances, though, the voice was not just personal but too casual.

Getting Feedback from Others

If you worry that the piece of writing you are working on is too personal for academic and professional writing, ask a few colleagues to read it for you.

- Rather than raise the issue directly, simply ask for comments in general. If you've been judicious in your use of the personal, your readers may not even see it as an issue. But once you bring it up, they may respond in terms of what they think is allowable rather than in terms of what works for them as readers.
- If you've written your first draft in a personal voice and now want to "professionalize" it without making it overly formal, ask a colleague or writing group to help you edit the first few pages. Once you see the ways they edit sentences to moderate the personal element, you can go through the rest of the draft and do the same thing yourself.

Writing on Your Own

The issue of whether and how to blend the personal and the professional is one that affects some writers more than others. In a discipline or profession that encourages a wide range of voices and rhetorical approaches, you may be free to try out several different voices and see which one(s) are most comfortable for you. However, the problem gets more challenging if your field is narrower and more conservative and if you feel strongly about the value of a personal voice.

- In your own reading and research, look for examples of academic or professional writing that strike you as having achieved a good balance of the personal and professional—voices that you might like to emulate in your own writing. When you sit down to write, have those models on hand, and stop to read them from time to time.
- If you find yourself consciously avoiding any mention of the personal in your professional writing, ask yourself why you are doing it. If it's because you're not comfortable with it, that's fine. However, if it's only because you think you shouldn't, it might be worth re-examining your assumptions.
- If you don't have others who can read your work and tell you whether you have struck the right balance of the personal and the professional, your best ally, as always, is time and distance. Setting aside a draft for even a couple of days may give you the perspective you need in order to judge whether you have achieved the right balance.
- If a reviewer or editor reacts negatively to your use of personal voice or anecdotes, don't automatically assume that you have no room to negotiate. Explain why you think the personal aspects are important, and ask the editor if he or she would be willing to read a version in which you tone down the personal but don't take it out completely.
- If you decide you want to challenge the professional norms in your field (for instance, to use first-person pronouns when they are not usually accepted in a particular journal), explain your choice explicitly in the text, in a footnote, or in your cover letter to the editor. If the editor sees that you have made the choice deliberately and explained your reasons for it, she may allow it to stand.

Scenario 4: Keeping It Under Control

Is there such a thing as too much voice in a piece of writing? Of course, although it's a bit of a rarity in academic and professional writing. In the writing groups I work with, excesses of voice usually occur in early drafts, indicating that the writer may have gotten caught up in the writing process. Perhaps he feels strongly about the topic and simply needs to get his feelings out before he can rein them in again. Or maybe he has learned from past experience that to try to control the voice early in the process is to shut down the flow of writing altogether. For the most part, writing with too much voice is easier to deal with than dull, lifeless prose. But when it does occur, it may turn out to be a cover for more serious problems.

Completely committed to his scholarly research, Kurt has spent years laboring in obscurity, loving his work but struggling to find an outlet for publication. Now, with recent world events focusing media attention on his topic, a major journal has announced plans to publish a special issue in the coming year. It's the perfect opportunity for Kurt, who has only to dust off some unpublished research, link it with recent events, and meet the announced deadline for submissions.

When he sends us the completed manuscript, he poses just two questions for us: (1) Do the new introduction and conclusion blend smoothly with the old material? and (2) Does he come off sounding too opinionated? Last year, Kurt tells us, an editor had asked him to cut a whole section of a book review because it sounded overly argumentative. And a paper he had sent out around the same time had been described by one reviewer as "more polemic than academic."

Kurt himself tended to regard the critiques as "epistemologically naive." He knew he had a tendency to get carried away in his passion for his subject. Still, he insisted that anyone claiming total objectivity on this politically charged topic was willfully blind to their own bias.

Kurt has begun by making just this point. Quoting at length from another writer's treatment of the subject, he shows how this author has misread the situation because of a failure to understand and acknowledge its political complexities. Before moving into his own analysis, he sketches out the particular theoretical perspective he will be bringing to the subject, distinguishing it from the two perspectives most typically adopted. Finally, he presents his own detailed analysis, relating it once again to the events that prompted the special issue.

In the writing group we begin by making several positive comments on Kurt's paper. We like the way he ties his research to the current events and see few problems with the transition from new material to old. We also like hearing Kurt's clear, forthright voice in the essay. Although we don't all share his sociopolitical perspective, we appreciate his frank acknowledgment of that perspective and his commitment to the notion that good scholarship involves reflective awareness of how ideas are situated.

Still, there is something about the essay that bothers us, and we suspect that it might have to do with Kurt's concern about sounding too opinionated. At first no one can name the problem, but as we continue to talk about the paper, two related issues emerge.

One issue has to do with the long section in which Kurt quotes and critiques the other author. Kurt's rebuttal of his argument sounds almost too easy—as if he were battling with the proverbial straw man. Sheepishly Kurt admits that there might be some truth in that. The other writer's views are not widely known, and they certainly aren't considered part of the mainstream. He is such an easy target, though, that Kurt couldn't resist demolishing him.

The second issue that emerges has to do with Kurt's choice of language. At one point he dismisses the prevailing interpretation of events as "simplistic," referring to his own theory as "the only reasonable explanation" for what occurred. Also he consistently refers to his own interpretations as if they are self-evident facts. One reader notices that three sentences on one page began with "Clearly"; someone else notices two appearances of "obviously" that don't seem all that obvious. In contrast Kurt labels opposing views as mere "claims" or "opinions," and twice comments on previous scholars' "failures" to account for certain things.

Reading Kurt's draft on our own, none of us had noticed *all* this loaded language, but each of us had noticed one or two examples that made us uncomfortable. Now when we join forces, even Kurt can see the cumulative effect. "It sounds like I don't have a case of my own," he says, "so I'm trying to bully the reader into taking my side."

Could this have been what the editor and reviewer meant when they cautioned Kurt about sounding too opinionated? At the time Kurt was sure that their critique derived from a theoretically unsound longing for objectivity—an interpretation that had the pleasing consolation of making him feel intellectually superior, even while he was being rejected. Now, though, he realizes he may have been wrong to dismiss their concern.

And now we realize that what we had praised as Kurt's "clear, forthright voice" may sound more like arrogance to some readers. Because we know Kurt as a fine and generous person, we regard his rhetorical excesses as natural exuberance. Perhaps in praising his passion and energy, we were doing him and his work a disservice.

We all have colleagues whose excesses of voice we enjoy, as well as others we find irritating or tiresome. In print these excesses are generally edited out, so we don't see them as often as we see their opposite: boring, lifeless prose. In some ways it's ironic that in professions placing so much value on academic freedom and on the rights of their members to speak out without fear of censure, conventions arise that constrain and "discipline" our exuberance. Or maybe that's just the point.

Getting Feedback from Others

When you're concerned about the voice or tone of a piece of writing, supportive readers can be an excellent sounding board. But remember, these can be subtle matters, and you may need to try several different approaches.

- If you are trying to establish a particular voice in your writing or to avoid an unwanted effect, one approach is to tell your friends or colleagues what you want them to look for as they read. Although you may be tempted to pose general questions, as Kurt did ("Do I sound too opinionated? Is the voice too informal? Too stuffy?"), this approach may encourage readers to give simple answers like "No, it's fine" or "Yes, it's stuffy." To get more specific feedback, you may need to ask more specific questions like these: "If you were the scholar whose work I'm critiquing in this section, would you feel I've treated your work respectfully?" or "The explanation of the issue on page six is supposed to be neutral and objective. Can you detect my personal bias at all?" If your friends or colleagues are at all hesitant to offer critical comments, questions like these may draw them out. By explaining what you're trying to do and then inviting specific responses, you are giving them permission to critique your work honestly and openly.

- Another way to use readers is to get them to do what we did with Kurt: circle any language that seems false, intemperate, inappropriate, and so forth. They don't even need to explain why. When you see what they've circled, chances are you'll agree that some of it doesn't work. From there it's an easy task to revise, but you can always ask for suggestions if you want to.

Writing on Your Own

Finding the right voice and tone for a piece of writing is like finding the right pitch if you're a singer. In the beginning, you may use a tuning instrument of some sort (another reader), but eventually you'll need to develop your own ear.

In this case, as in the previous scenarios, "developing your ear" means paying attention to voice and tone in the reading you do for both work and for pleasure.

- When you find yourself noticing the voice or tone of a piece of writing, in either positive or negative ways, stop and ask yourself what accounts for your reaction. Focus particularly on the writer's language and sentence rhythms. This is where most voice and tone gets projected.

• If a piece catches your attention because of flaws in voice or tone (for example, it sounds too arrogant, too stuffy, too breezy), try editing it right there in the margins of the book or journal. Practicing editing for voice and tone in other people's work is a good way to train yourself to hear your own.

Is it possible to write in your own voice without sacrificing professional credibility? Absolutely. Even though readers of academic and professional writing expect to be addressed in a respectful, professional manner, they also appreciate hearing a human being behind the prose. If there is too much voice in a piece of writing—if you come on too strong or too breezy or too hesitant or too arrogant—you may alienate readers and lose academic credibility. But the opposite approach may be a problem as well. If you play it safe, take no risks, keep yourself separate and apart from your subject, you may lose potential readers of another kind. More important, you may lose touch with what motivated your work in the first place.

5

Seeing the Project Through

Sometimes the greatest challenges we face as writers are the challenges that lie within. Just finding time to write is a perennial problem for most of us, not to mention the blank page or screen that looms large in so many accounts of writer's block. Once a piece is under way, even the most experienced writer can stall out for any number of reasons. And some of us find that declaring something finished is the greatest challenge of all.

Facing and surmounting the inner obstacles that impede writing isn't easy, but it's reassuring to know that most writers, even famous ones, encounter the same difficulties we do. What is more sobering is to realize that despite the regular outpouring of articles on how to beat writer's block that appear in *Writer's Digest* and similar publications, no one seems to have a magic formula for how to get the work of writing done.

I don't have it either.

Still, I often find encouragement in the stories that come out of our writing group—stories of starting and stopping, of procrastinating and persisting, of giving up and going back and getting it done.

Scenario 1: Getting Started

Probably the most common problem all writers face is getting started. It's so common, in fact, that calling it a problem may be misleading.

It's more like a simple situation—a necessary part of the writing process that every writer faces and that most feel some anxiety about.

A few weeks ago Peter was contacted by the editor of a prominent journal in his discipline, asking if he would be willing to review a new book in his area of expertise. Because it was a book he planned to read anyway, he readily agreed to review it and signed up to bring his first draft to the writing group two weeks before the deadline.

When his writing group date arrives, however, Peter has virtually nothing to show us. Although he read the book over winter break and made plenty of notes, he is having a terrible time actually starting to write the review. It isn't for lack of time or opportunity. With his family away over part of the break, he had more than enough time to write. And it isn't for lack of ideas either; he has plenty to say about the book. At this point Peter isn't sure why he's not writing. He's just embarrassed and discouraged about it.

The rest of us are sympathetic. We have all found ourselves in similar situations, and we know how frustrating it can be. We offer various kinds of advice ("Just do it!" "Force yourself to write for fifteen minutes a day"), and we encourage Peter to talk about his ideas, hoping the talk will get him started. The next week, though, Peter is still battling his writing demons and worrying about what to tell the editor. And the week after that, all he has managed to do is negotiate a one-month extension.

Finally, after several weeks and more extensions, Peter arrives at our weekly meeting with a six-page draft in hand. If we have time, he says, he would like us to read it. However, the piece is once again overdue, and he has promised to send it off this week, so there is little time to revise.

Fortunately, we see little need for revision. The review Peter gives us, though brief, is thoughtful, clear, and well written; the minor changes we suggest can be easily made. As we're packing up to go, someone asks Peter what finally got him started, and he stops to give it some thought.

Last week he was cleaning out some old files when he ran across the notes he had made for a conference presentation last year. As he glanced through them, feeling guilty about not having done anything with them since, he realized that he could use some of this material for his book review. The next day he found himself thinking about the review while he sat through a boring department meeting. Just to keep himself occupied, he scribbled a couple of notes on the back of the meeting agenda, and before he knew it, he was jotting a rough outline for the whole review. That afternoon while driving home, the perfect opening sentence popped into his head. When he got home, he went immediately to his study to write it down and just kept going from there.

What was it that got Peter started writing on this project? In this case it seemed to be serendipity as much as anything else. If he hadn't been cleaning out his files that day, if he hadn't found those notes, if the department meeting had been more interesting, or if he had had company on the ride home—if any of these things had happened, Peter might still be asking his editor for one more extension. But Peter himself can take a little credit, too, for requesting the extension in the first place, for noticing the connection between his old notes and the book he was reviewing, for letting his mind wander in productive directions during the department meeting, and for seizing the opportunity to write down that sentence when it came to him unbidden.

Of course, trusting in serendipity isn't always the best solution to writer's block. Sometimes we need more systematic ways of getting past the blank page, and numerous books and articles offer advice on that subject. (See Appendix C for one such book that is aimed primarily at academics.)

For other writers it may be simply a matter of "accepting the block" and moving on. Psycholinguist Frank Smith makes this point in his book, *Writing and the Writer* (1982):

> All kinds of people write. What distinguishes the writers is not that they have hearts of stone and minds of steel. They probably run the range of anxieties and writing blocks as much as nonwriters. The main difference is that they write. They live with their uncertainties and difficulties, and they write. [p. 134]

Whether you work systematically or depend on intuition and serendipity, it is important to know yourself as a writer—to recognize the barriers that impede your writing and the factors that help you succeed. To acquire such self-knowledge isn't easy, of course. It requires facing up to habits of procrastination, self-doubt, and rationalization that we all suffer from. But it also requires acknowledging strengths. We're all professionals; we got where we are by succeeding more often than we failed. Paying attention to the strengths, techniques, and habits of mind that helped us thrive in the past builds the confidence we need when we take on new writing projects.

Getting Feedback from Others

Whether you consider yourself a blocked writer or simply a procrastinator, it is good to have colleagues to help you get started writing. Some people in our writing groups say that just having to bring something to the group on a given day has proven to be a powerful incentive to write. (For that reason, it's good to make this a regular expectation in the group. See Appendix A.) But sometimes the deadline in itself isn't quite enough. Whether you have a regular group to work with or just a willing friend or office partner to read your work, consider one of these ways to enlist others in your cause:

• Ask a couple of friends or colleagues if you can sit down and talk through a project with them. Sometimes their interest in a particular aspect of your topic may be just the spark you need to start writing.

- Show them an outline of your paper and ask for feedback on the overall plan. For some people, writing outlines is less intimidating than writing sentences, and the simple act of getting words on paper can break through the inertia barrier. (Beware, though, if you tend to use making outlines as a way to put off the actual writing. I must have outlined my dissertation half a dozen times before my adviser made me stop planning and write!)
- Ask your friends or colleagues to read just one page or one paragraph or one sentence—whatever it takes to get you to write something down. If you know you only have to write one page, you may find yourself writing five in spite of yourself.

When you give your colleagues something to read, ask yourself what you want or need from them. For instance, you might simply want your readers to show an interest in your project. That way they can be the human faces that you imagine in your audience as you write. If it's discipline you need, your colleagues can be tough task masters as well. They may not be comfortable in this role at first, but if you give them permission and tell them this is what you want, they will probably warm to the role.

Writing on Your Own

One way of getting to know yourself as a writer is to visualize yourself writing successfully. For every writer it's different, of course, but here are some things you might think about:

Time

Some writers need deadlines, and they work best under pressure. The more time they have, the more they waste. The less they have, the more efficient they become. If you're one of these people, you may need to set some deadlines for yourself; better yet, force someone else to set some deadlines for you. If you need lots of time and less pressure, you'll have to find some way of carving it out of your busy schedule. For me the most productive times to write have always been summers, and I try to keep them as free from other commitments as I can. Other writers I know get up early and spend two hours writing before the rest of the family gets up. Or else they cross one day of the week off their calendars and resolutely refuse to schedule appointments or classes on that day. All this presumes, of course, that you have control over your schedule, and not everyone does. But you may have more control than you realize. For instance, all of us who teach classes necessarily rule out appointments and committee meetings during the times when we are in class. Why not schedule a regular writing time and commit to it just as firmly? At first it may be hard to do because some hours will feel very unproductive. But that's to be expected. We all have unproductive class sessions, too, but that doesn't mean we cancel the whole course.

Space

Some writers work best in cluttered offices—the mess on their desks a symbolic representation, perhaps, of the rich chaos of ideas in their heads. Others need a clear space and as few distractions as possible. As with time, we don't always have control over what space we work in, but there are still decisions to be made. When I began this book, I made a spontaneous decision not to work in my office, where I do nearly all my writing on the computer. Instead I sat out on the deck one day after breakfast and just wrote. When the stories started coming, I realized that not being in my office had something to do with my productivity. As I continued to write, I sought out places that felt good—sunny chairs in the living room, coffee shops downtown—so that I could take advantage of the mental space they seemed to create in my head.

Voices

I'm not sure how many academic writers would say they listen for voices in their heads. But that's the metaphor I use to explain the sudden appearance of a sentence or part of a sentence that gets me started writing. Peter heard "voices" as he was driving home that day: language forming in his head, working at some subconscious level on the material he had been accumulating. For many writers these voices come at predictable times: when they're drifting off to sleep or waking up, when they're jogging or showering or washing dishes. Once you learn to recognize the times when the voices in your head are likely to speak, make sure you have a pad and pen nearby.

The Right Stuff

I know it sounds trivial, but having the right stuff—the right pen, the right paper, the right lamp, the right music, the right drink, the right snack, the right chair—all these can help you break the iner-tia barrier. When I began writing this book, the right stuff was two tablets of grid paper from Levenger—a recent gift from my husband. I don't know why those tablets seemed so important. Maybe it was the doodle room they afforded me. But they got me writing one morning, and they kept me writing for several weeks as I worked on the first draft of this book.

If all else fails, it's good to remember this often-quoted line at-tributed to writer Gene Fowler: "Writing is easy. All you do is stare at a blank sheet of paper until drops of blood form on your forehead."

Scenario 2: Learning to Like Revising

By the time we finish graduate school, most of us are well aware of the importance of revision. We see it as a normal and essential part of the writing process and know that we must allow ourselves plenty of time to do it, both while we are writing and after we have gotten some perspective on a first draft.

But knowing that revision is necessary and normal doesn't nec-essarily make it easier to do. For revision is rarely the simple editing process we might like it to be. More often, it raises issues we had hoped were settled, requiring us to generate new language, devise new rhetorical strategies, and even reconstruct meaning.

Although revision is generally an accepted part of the process for experienced writers, in the writing groups I work with I have noticed at least two circumstances in which faculty writers resist revising as stubbornly as students do: (1) when the revision entails letting go of work the writer doesn't want to let go of and (2) when the revision is being done at the behest of an unknown reviewer or editor. When these two conditions occur at the same time, as they occasionally do, that normal and essential part of the writing process can become a major sticking point for the writer.

Ever since Gina first heard that her book was accepted by a major academic press, she has been excited about getting back to work on the revisions her editor asked for. Most of the editor's comments and suggestions have been easy to deal with, but the fourth chapter presents a more complicated problem.

In the editor's view, some of the material in that chapter overlaps too much with the content of earlier chapters. Most of his marginal comments occur about five pages into the chapter, so that's where Gina has focused her attention.

When she sends the chapter to the writing group, Gina includes a copy of the editor's comments, and when we meet to talk about her work, she tells us how discouraged she feels.

"He obviously doesn't like this section," she says, "but I don't know what to do about it. The sad thing is that it was my favorite part of the chapter. I was really on a roll when I was writing it, and I love the way it turned out."

"I like this section, too," one group member comments, "but I can see the editor's point. It does cover some of the same ground you covered in Chapter Two. Could you move it back there as he suggests?"

"That won't work," says Gina. "This section also draws on ideas that don't come up until Chapter Three."

"Then use it there," someone else suggests.

"I tried that," says Gina. "It throws the whole chapter off."

For a while we try making other suggestions, but none of them seem to work for Gina. After an hour or so we find ourselves feeling as frustrated as she is.

At that point I make the kind of suggestion I know writers hate to hear: "Maybe it would help to sit down in front of a blank screen and just start this chapter over."

Start over after all this work? Gina's expression reveals exactly what she thinks of that idea. For her, writing never comes easily, and throwing out a whole section that took hours to write seems like a huge waste of time and effort. Besides, she's still not convinced that this section has to come out.

"You don't have to throw it out completely," I tell her. "Just set it aside for a while and let yourself write. And don't worry about losing all that work. Starting over with a blank screen doesn't mean starting with a blank mind. The work you did is still in your head in some form."

Gina is still not convinced. "You may be right," she says. "But I just can't bring myself to do it."

Over the next few weeks Gina works on her revision, avoiding the problematic chapter. At one point, she tells us she may just leave it as is and see if the editor notices. But then she decides she can't take that risk and determines, as a last resort, to try my "blank screen approach."

At our meeting the next week, she tells us how it worked. Instead of calling up the existing draft on her computer and trying to revise from the problem point on page five, she opened a brand new file and started drafting the chapter from scratch. Although the writing didn't come easily at first, it started to move more smoothly once she got past the new opening paragraph. In fact, after she got going, she started to like the new approach she was taking. And after a few pages she reached a point where she could open the old file, copy the last half of the original chapter, and merge the two together quite smoothly.

"What happened to that section you didn't want to change?" someone in the group asks.

"Oh, I had to leave it out," Gina says. "But that's all right. The chapter works much better without it."

Learning how to let go is often difficult for writers, especially when we aren't fully convinced that letting go of what we have written is necessary. In Gina's case the situation was complicated by the fact that she didn't quite trust her editor's judgment. Having produced a piece of writing she liked, she was loathe to "waste" all the time and energy she had invested in it just because the editor had problems with it. The fact that the group agreed with the editor may have been discouraging at first, but eventually it allowed Gina to see the wisdom of the editor's suggestion.

Dealing with comments from reviewers and editors is seldom a purely positive experience, even when that feedback is generally affirmative. Despite the editor's best intentions, it often puts us into a defensive posture, reminding us what it felt like to be a powerless graduate student. In many cases, though, there is more room to negotiate than we realize. Good editors regard it as part of their job to work with writers and will generally be happy to respond to calls or e-mail questions. (My own preference is for e-mail, because it gives the other person time to locate and reread your manuscript before responding.) If you're not sure about an editor's comments (maybe you can't tell whether you are being encouraged to revise or just let down gently), don't hesitate to ask your question directly. Nor should you hesitate to press back a little on issues about which you feel strongly (for example, "I understand why you objected to that paragraph on page three, but I think the point is an important one. Would you be open to a revision that . . . ?") As long as you make it clear that you respect the editor's judgment and that your only interest is in improving the manuscript, there is no harm in pursuing the matter.

Getting Feedback from Others

If you get reviewer feedback that you find yourself resisting or just not understanding, ask a couple of trusted friends or colleagues to read the comments and tell you what they think. (This works best, of course, if the friends or colleagues have read the manuscript in question, but it's not always necessary.) Because they are less attached to your work than you are but on your side nonetheless, honest, supportive readers can help you sort through, interpret, and respond to the feedback you've been given. Here are some suggestions:

- If the editor or reviewer makes comments you don't understand or suggests revisions you don't want to make, supportive readers can help you hear what you need to hear and respond to those suggestions less defensively than you otherwise might. Share a copy of the comments with your readers, and ask them to help you figure out what to do.
- If an editor sends reviewer comments that seem conflicting or even contradictory and leaves it to you to revise as you see fit, ask your readers to help you strategize. In some cases neutral readers may see ways to satisfy both reviewers by devising some changes that address the underlying problems in the draft rather than the surface manifestations the reviewers have reacted to.
- If a reviewer has completely misread your manuscript or is uninterested in the work you are doing, let yourself blow off steam to your colleagues. They can help you shrug off those comments and focus your energies more positively.
- If you find yourself so fixated on the negative comments that you overlook the editor's encouragement to revise and resubmit, your readers can reinforce the positive comments and make sure you don't give up too soon.

Sharing reviewer comments with others may be hard to do at first, especially if some of the comments are particularly stinging, but learning to develop a thick skin is necessary for every academic writer.

Writing on Your Own

Deciding to let go of work you have written is always hard, but it gets easier the more you do it. Here are some suggestions for how to make it a little less painful:

- First, decide what has to go and why. Was something wrong with the way you began the piece, or does it get off track later on? It's not always easy to determine this, as Gina's situation illustrates.
- Now set aside everything you've written after that point. Notice I say "set aside," not "throw away." You may feel tempted to delete a whole file or tear up a draft, but the momentary catharsis probably isn't worth the cost of losing some good material.
- Unless you're wholly committed to revising, you may find that the old material keeps whispering to you, trying to persuade you that it wasn't so bad after all. Resist its siren call. Unless you get as far away from the old material as possible, it will be like trying to hum one tune with another playing loudly in the background. You may think you're doing it successfully, but everyone else knows you're off key.
- Once you start drafting new material, keep going. Chances are you will realize as you write that some of what you want to say is back in that original draft. Don't go looking for it. Just leave some space, make a note to yourself ("use old definition here"), and keep writing. That way you won't lose continuity, and you won't get distracted by the old material that doesn't fit in so well.
- At some point you may find, as Gina did, that you have written yourself out of the problem and can now merge your new material with the previous draft. At that point you'll need to smooth in some transitions and make sure the seams don't show.

- Finally, if you find that you've written all the way through a new draft *without* thinking of the old material, that's fine. It means you probably won't have much smoothing of seams to do later on. Still, it's a good idea to review the old material just to make sure you haven't forgotten something important.

Scenario 3: Getting It in the Mail

For some writers, *finishing* a piece of writing may be as difficult as getting started in the first place. This is especially true for writers who have a bit of the perfectionist in them. But it may be a problem for procrastinators of other kinds as well.

For Michael, a perfectionist if there ever was one, actually finishing a piece of writing is almost impossible to imagine. Always there is more to add to a piece. Always there is something further to work on.

Last fall when Michael brought his research article to our writing group, we thought it was very close to being finished. A couple of readers had questions or comments on content and organization, but most of us had little to say beyond a few suggestions for editing and polishing sentences.

At the time Michael had thanked us for our comments and suggestions and said he hoped to get the piece in the mail very shortly. Two months later, though, we learn that he has still not mailed it off. Why not?

Michael has his reasons. For one thing he has decided he needs to do a little more reading on the theoretical basis for his research. A new book came out just last semester that he really couldn't ignore, and in it he found references to a whole subfield of work he was not familiar with. He is also not that happy with the discussion section of his paper. He knows we like it, and he values our opinions, but when he asked for some feedback from a colleague in his department, she said she thought he had overstated his conclusions. Finally, he's still not satisfied with the style of the piece. When he went back to make the sentence-level revisions that we had suggested earlier, he found that the changes he made created other kinds of problems, and now the piece doesn't seem to flow as well.

We aren't entirely surprised. Michael is clearly the kind of writer who takes great pains with his work. We see that in his excellent critiques of our papers, on which he offers profuse comments, and he's told us about the hours he spends with his grad students' dissertations and theses. Eventually, we know, Michael will get that paper in the mail, and when he does we have every confidence that it will be accepted, probably without major revisions. But in the meantime, there's another issue we need to address.

Next year Michael is up for promotion. This will be his second try. Last year when he came up automatically after six years in rank, his department supported him on the basis of his superb teaching and the soundness of his scholarly work. But the college and university committees regretfully turned him down. They too respected his teaching and his scholarly work, but his record of publication was a little thin. If he could just get a couple more pieces out, they said, they would have no trouble supporting him.

Despite the warning, however, Michael has not been able to "get a couple more pieces out." Instead, he has worked on this one paper constantly, convinced that unless he hones it to a state of perfection, it will be rejected and he will lose valuable time trying to place it in another journal.

Michael's strategy made sense when he first told us this, nearly a year ago, but now we are all wondering if he has a death wish of some sort. Is it fear of failure? Fear of success? Why won't he put it in the mail?

We are all feeling frustrated until someone says, "Look, if you had infinite time, maybe you could read every book on this subject and polish every sentence to perfection. But the fact is, you don't have infinite time. If you've overstated the conclusions, put in some qualifiers. But then get the thing in the mail. We can't afford to lose you!"

For some reason this pep talk seems to work. Maybe it's just because Michael is finally ready to hear it. Maybe it's because no one has said it quite this way before. At any rate Michael reports next time that he mailed the piece out over the weekend. If he hadn't, we were ready to walk him to the post office and buy him the stamps!

Getting Feedback from Others

If you have trouble declaring a project finished and getting it in the mail, a writing group can be your best friend—or your worst enemy. And the same goes for individual friends or partners who agree to read your work and give you feedback.

- Unless they know you well, your readers may not recognize your tendency toward perfectionism or your simple fear of failure. Without realizing it they can even contribute to the problem by writing more and more comments on more and more drafts, thus giving you all the excuses you need to keep working on your project indefinitely. If you know you're a perfectionist, don't keep asking for additional feedback.

- Once your readers understand how you work, they can help you bring your writing to closure. If you want their help, just ask them directly. "Do you think this is ready to send out yet?" If they know you want an honest answer, they'll give it to you.

Writing on Your Own

Here is another instance in which going it alone can be part of the problem you're facing. If you don't have a group or a friend to help you make the big leap, you may need to train yourself for that role.

- Instead of asking yourself if you've covered everything, ask yourself if the piece you've written feels reasonably complete. We all know the answer to the first question. The second one is more likely to get a realistic answer.

- Instead of thinking of all the published books and articles that are so much better than yours, think of all the ones that are worse. Don't be modest. You know you've read published work that didn't measure up to your standards. If it found its way into print, why shouldn't yours?

- Remember that many pieces you see in print went through the "revise and resubmit" process first. If there's potential in your manuscript, trust a good editor to see it and help you improve the piece.

- Realize that no matter how perfectly you polish your writing, the editor is probably going to want you to change things. The less you obsess at this point, the less disappointed you'll be when you see what you're asked to change.

Getting started is often the hardest part of the writing process, but declaring a project finished can be just as difficult. And along the way there may be numerous challenges and temptations to abandon the work in progress. That's why the most successful writers are the ones who know themselves best. Systematic people develop systems. Intuitive people develop intuitive approaches. In the long run, though, it's best to have a wide range of strategies, as well as deep reserves of patience and perseverance to see you through.

Afterword

We've all heard the usual advice about writing introductions and conclusions: "Tell 'em what you're going to tell 'em. Then tell 'em what you told 'em." Like all conventional wisdom it makes a certain amount of sense. Telling readers where you're headed allows them to relax and enjoy the journey. And summing up what you've just said gives them something to take away with them.

If I were to heed this conventional advice, I would conclude by re-emphasizing two simple but important points:

- *Think always in terms of purpose and audience.* What are you trying to accomplish with this piece of writing? Who will most likely be reading it? How can you anticipate the needs of your readers and help them follow what you have to say?

- *Find an engaging professional voice—one that conveys your interest in your subject.* If you write in a voice that feels comfortable to *you*, you're more likely to produce writing that others will want to read.

That's not everything of course. It leaves out many of the details. But that's what conclusions are supposed to do, isn't it? They wrap things up and boil things down and explain what it all adds up to.

Maybe that's why I dislike conclusions. They seem so reductive.
For as soon as I write those two pieces of advice, I want to qualify and complicate them. I want to say that we sometimes have to start writing before we know exactly what we want to say, that it's sometimes our hyperawareness of audience that alienates us from our own voices, that some readers aren't as receptive to "engaging voices" as we might like them to be.

For a while this frustration with conclusions made me resist writing one altogether. When I mentioned this in my faculty writing group, a colleague suggested a way around the dilemma. "Don't call it a conclusion," he said. "Call it concluding remarks or afterword." I liked that idea. In an afterword you don't have to just "tell 'em what you told 'em" in some dry, mechanical way. You can write in your own voice, say what you want to say, resist the pressure to simplify. As soon as I typed "afterword" at the top of the page, I could sit down and write.

I tell you this story now because it offers one more example of the importance of finding your voice—and also because it illustrates the unpredictable quirkiness of writing, that elusive aspect of our work that keeps us intrigued by the process.

Appendix A:
Organizing a Writing Group

In her book *Writing Groups: History, Theory, and Implications*, Anne Ruggles Gere shares some interesting information about writing groups as an American cultural and historical phenomenon, both within and outside academic institutions. "As the history of writing groups in this country illustrates," she says, "there is no one 'right' way to proceed" (p. 99).

> Groups range in size from three to forty. . . . Some groups exchange written drafts and receive verbal or written comments, while some read aloud and receive oral response. Some shift the procedure to suit the material (reading long essays or poems and listening to shorter prose selections, for example). Groups observe differing codes for response. Some intervene directly in members' writing—helping generate ideas or telling the writer what to do next—while others restrict responses to what has already been written. [Gere, 1987, p. 1]

Although each writing group has its own purposes and necessarily reflects its members' interests and personalities, it may be useful to see a detailed example of how one kind of academic writing group works. For that reason I include here a description of the basic plan we have followed in the faculty and graduate student writing groups

I have worked with over the years. My purpose is not to suggest that this pattern works best for academic and professional writers or that it is appropriate—or even desirable—in all situations. Rather, my purpose is to offer some ideas to work from—ideas you can adopt, adapt, revise, or reject if you are planning a group of your own.

Basic Structure

Our writing groups all begin with a core group of people (generally between six and twelve) who commit to meeting for an hour once a week for a full fifteen-week semester. At the beginning of the semester we all bring our calendars, and each of us signs up for one or two dates. The week before our date we send out to each member of the group a piece of our writing in progress, along with a cover sheet explaining the context and asking particular questions. When the group meets, we go through a regular routine, giving the writer spoken feedback on the work. At the end of the session we may also hand over our written comments, depending on whether or not we think they will be useful to the writer.

Membership

When our writing groups first began, they were part of a grant-funded Writing Across the Curriculum program. At that time faculty had to apply and get their dean's recommendation to participate. The idea behind this was that faculty would be more likely to honor a commitment to the group if they felt that the dean was aware of their participation, and in some cases we know this strategy worked.

These days, however, our approach tends to be less formal. Early in the semester we post a notice in the university newsletter and send a mailing to all faculty, announcing the time of this semester's faculty writing group and inviting expressions of interest. The meeting time is usually the deciding factor. We rarely find a time when more than ten to twelve faculty are free.

In some cases writing groups have continued past the one-semester term. One group I currently belong to has been in existence for over six years, its membership shifting occasionally as someone leaves and a new person is drafted to join us. In this case the decision about who to invite is a group decision. Given the longevity of this group, it's important that anyone new "fit in."

Meetings

We meet every week at the same time. Or at least we commit to that schedule. Sometimes, especially with smaller groups, we may skip a week if no one has a piece of writing to bring, but over the years we have found that having an alternate-week schedule or varying our meeting day and time just creates confusion for us. It's easier to know that every Tuesday at 4:00 P.M. is writing group time, and making a commitment to that time helps us all make a commitment to the group.

Even with the regular meeting time, we have found it useful to send reminders to everyone the day before the group meets. Usually that is the leader's responsibility, but if we have a voice-mail or e-mail list set up for the group, anyone can post a message to the rest of the group.

When we start out, our groups meet in classrooms—preferably seminar rooms where we can all gather around a common table. This academic atmosphere makes us take our work seriously, and it gives us the quiet we need to do our work. In the six-year-old continuing group, we are all comfortable with each other now, so we have moved to a campus coffee shop where there is a quiet side room we can use at the end of the day.

Leadership

It is important that each group have a leader who will be responsible for setting up the schedule, keeping people informed of changes, and, most important, keeping the group on track when work is being discussed. I've always argued that it doesn't matter whether the leader is a "writing person" or not. In some cases "writing people" can really inhibit a group. What is most important is that the leader is well organized, good humored, and firm but flexible in his or her determination to keep the group on track. It's easy to err on either side of this firm-to-flexible continuum. If the leader is too flexible, the group may lose its sense of purpose along with its structure. If he or she is too firm, the structure can actually get in the way of the group.

Routine

Because time is of the essence, we always follow a simple routine that keeps us focused on our work. When a group is forming, I generally explain this routine, distribute a handout that explains the writer's role and the readers' role (see Exhibits 1 and 2), and suggest that we try it for a couple of weeks to see what we think. Usually we continue to follow the routine throughout the semester, though we may make adaptations as we go along.

The routine that has evolved over the years has four basic parts. First, we see if anyone has questions about the purpose, intended audience, and context of the piece. Although we ask the writer to explain this on the cover sheet, we often need to clear up additional questions.

Then we move to the all-important "positive comments round" in which each member of the group, in turn, makes one specific, positive comment on the piece. We have found this to be absolutely essential for building trust. Academics tend to be critical by nature, and if we leap to critical comments without first acknowledging what we like about a piece of writing, we risk losing that important sense of trust.

After the positive comments round we turn to the questions the writer has raised about the piece. This too is very important. In most cases the writer has a good sense of what problems need to be addressed. But even when the writer seems to be asking the wrong

Exhibit 1. Writer's Responsibilities

1. As the writer, your first responsibility is to give us a readable draft. Since our time is limited, and since we are all from different fields, we can't really handle book manuscripts or full-length articles in technical fields, but if we are adequately prepared by the writer, we can probably deal reasonably with opening chapters or short sections of difficult material—and we may be able to handle somewhat longer pieces of work intended for more general audiences. Some people may bring very early draft work and others bring near-final drafts. As long as we know what we're reading, we can give useful responses.

2. When you prepare your draft, be sure to attach a cover sheet in which you explain what the piece of writing is, what audience it is intended for, what your format constraints are, what draft stage it's in, and what *particular questions* you would like us to address. It's important to be as specific as possible here in order to focus our attention on the issues you see as most important. Remember that we don't know your field or its research and publishing conventions. If you use specialized terms in the paper, and if it's not too much trouble, it might be a good idea to briefly define key terms on your cover sheet.

3. Have your draft ready to distribute to the group *the week before* your sign-up date. You can always tell us a little about the piece when you hand it out, but we'll still need the cover sheet to refer to later. If any group members are missing when you distribute your paper, be sure to send them a copy in intercampus mail.

4. When we're discussing your work, your role will be primarily to listen and take notes. This isn't always easy. You may want to explain, argue, defend your choices rather than simply absorb responses. (And you may find that we get so interested in your topic that we all get "off task.") That's okay from time to time, but usually, it's best to listen more than you talk. Remember: it's *your* work and *you* are the final arbiter. No one will ask you to bring in your next version and reveal which comments you used and which you ignored. (If you *want* to bring in a revised version, however, either to have us read again or just to share with us, that's fine.)

University Writing Program
University of North Dakota

Exhibit 2. Readers' Responsibilities

1. Our first responsibility as readers is to take time to read carefully and generously. Our purpose is to help the writer prepare this piece of writing for its intended audience, so it's important to read the cover sheet and keep the writer's audience in mind as we read and respond.

It's also a good idea to read with a hierarchy of concerns in mind. If it's an early draft, don't get hung-up on sentence-level editorial suggestions; if it's a final draft going in the mail next week, don't suggest starting over with a whole new approach. [See Exhibit 3 for more on this.]

2. For the most part, our comments will be made orally, in the group meeting. However, if you made written comments on your copy of the draft that you think might be useful to the writer, feel free to hand those over at the end of the meeting. (And if you have to miss a meeting, that's a good way to give the writer your responses to his/her work.)

3. We'll start each session with a *clarification round*. This is a chance to clear up any general questions we might have before going on to focus on the particulars of the piece. (For instance, we might need to ask something about the intended audience or make sure we understand the meaning of a key term or concept.)

4. Next comes the *positive comment round*. Because it's so easy to feel defensive about work we've invested a lot of time and energy in, we always begin by asking each person to comment specifically on one thing they liked or admired about the piece. Positive comments may be on content, organization, voice, style—any aspect of the writing that you care to single out. *Do try to be relatively specific*, though. "I liked it—it's good" doesn't tell the writer much about what she or he is doing well. Don't worry if you are the last to be called on and your comment has already been noted by someone else. If more than one person likes the same thing, that's especially powerful reinforcement.

5. After positive comments from everyone, we turn to *the writer's questions*. On the cover sheet, the writer will have posed some questions that he or she would particularly like us to respond to, for example: "Is the transition from section I to section II too abrupt?" "Have I explained antidisestablishmentarianism thoroughly enough?" "Do I sound

defensive?" Even if you think other questions are more central, try to have something brief to say about the questions the writer has raised.

6. Once we've responded to the writer's questions, we'll go on to mention *other comments, questions, suggestions* we have for the writer.
As always, we'll want to keep a positive tone and make sure the writer knows that even critical comments are delivered in the spirit of helpful feedback.

University Writing Program
University of North Dakota

questions, addressing those questions first shows that we respect the writer's ownership of the work.

After we have addressed the questions the writer raises, we are free to bring up other issues. Generally speaking, we try to keep these to a minimum unless those other issues are really crucial or there is plenty of time left over to talk. Unless we're careful, we can overwhelm the writer with too much feedback coming from too many directions.

Levels of Response

In addition to the basic routine, I also bring to each new group some suggestions about what to focus on when we read each other's drafts (see Exhibit 3). These suggestions grow out of my own experience as a writing teacher and as a supervisor of graduate teaching assistants who are just learning to read and respond to student writing.

In all of these situations, readers can find themselves zeroing in on what we call sentence-level aspects of writing, often at the expense of deeper and more complex rhetorical issues. What I try to do with this handout is to sketch out three different levels at which we may approach a piece of writing. Even though all three levels

Exhibit 3. Reading Drafts in Progress: Levels of Response

It is often useful, when responding to drafts, to think in terms of a hierarchy of concerns, beginning with large-scale matters like focus and overall tone and moving toward sentence-level editing and proofreading. If a draft is in early form, the writer will probably want to focus on large-scale concerns first. If it's in a late draft stage, it may be ready for sentence-level editing. Be sure to notice what stage the draft is in (it will be noted on the cover sheet) and offer feedback appropriately.

I. Large-scale concerns

Is the purpose of the piece clear?
Does it seem to be appropriate for its intended audience?
Are the ideas explained fully enough?
Is the form consistent with expected professional/academic guidelines?
Are the overall voice and tone appropriate (e.g., neither too formal nor too casual)?

II. Mid-level concerns

Is the order of ideas logical? Does anything seem to be out of place?
Are section and paragraph breaks logical and appropriate?
Are the transitions between sections or ideas smooth?
Are there enough signposts and subheadings to help the reader through the piece?

III. Sentence-level concerns

Are sentences clear and mechanically correct?
Any misused words or awkward phrases?
Is punctuation used appropriately and effectively?
Could the language be made more concise or precise?
Could the language be made more active and lively?

University Writing Program
University of North Dakota

are important, it is usually best not to try to address them all at once. Rather, we need to consider what stage of the writing process the writer is in and what kind of feedback is most needed at this point. If the writer is still in the early stages of figuring out what he or she wants to say, there is little use in offering suggestions on wording or sentence structure. By the same token if the piece has to go in the mail tomorrow, it's probably not the time to suggest a major recon-ceptualization.

Talk

One semester when I was on leave, a colleague volunteered to lead a new faculty writing group. To build in some accountability, she set it up so that everyone had to submit at least one revised version of an earlier draft the group had read. Otherwise she ran the group pretty much as it had been done before.

When I saw her the next semester, she wanted to talk about the experience. "It was a disaster!" she said. The group had started with ten but by the end of the semester, only three or four were still meeting. What had she done wrong?

Probably she had done nothing wrong. Sometimes a group just doesn't click, and there may be nothing you can do to save it. Still, I found myself wondering about that revision expectation. Could it have made the faculty want to avoid returning to the group?

As a writing teacher, I've seen this happen with students: if the teacher comes on too strong, reading a draft one way and pushing it in a certain direction, the student may balk and back away from it. If the teacher does that all semester long, the student may back away for good.

When we read our colleagues' writing, the same thing can hap-pen. We may sometimes get so caught up in a piece that we come on too strong, telling our colleague what to do instead of offering helpful observations and suggestions. In the groups I work with, no one is obligated to show us their revision, and that seems to work out well. People feel free to pick and choose the comments they find most helpful, and no one's feelings are hurt because their own suggestions weren't used in the next draft.

At the same time we also work on couching our critical comments in language the writer can hear. Here's a sample of what I mean:

I wonder if you've considered . . . .

I realize I'm not your intended audience here, but . . . .

Here's one suggestion. I don't know if it would work, but it might be worth a try.

If this were my essay—and I realize that it isn't—I might . . . .

You're going to hate me for saying this, but . . . .

It's possible that I've misread this, but . . . .

When the writer is particularly sensitive or when everyone is tiptoeing around a problem, it's especially hard but just as important to offer helpful critical comments. In those situations I often find myself taking a deep breath and saying, "OK, I'll be the bad guy today" or "Shall I offer a minority report?"

Finally, learning to laugh at ourselves, both as writers and readers, is one of the most important things we can do to make the feedback process productive. The leader of the group can set an important tone here, bringing in his or her own work and responding with good humor to the comments that are made.

Progress Reports

Although we don't expect writers to bring their revised drafts to the group, we are all interested in hearing follow-up reports of what has happened to a piece of writing since we last saw it. For that reason we occasionally set aside time for progress reports—a few minutes at the beginning of a session when everyone reports on what they have done with their writing since we last saw it. If someone has had a piece accepted for publication or perhaps has just broken through a particularly frustrating writing block, we have a chance to celebrate. If the report is less positive—if an article, for example, has been rejected or set aside or if the writer is feeling discouraged about it—we use the occasion to offer encouragement and support.

In our continuing groups the first meeting of a new semester is a good time for these progress reports. Usually we don't have a piece to read yet, so we use that meeting to sign up for dates and catch up on what everyone is doing.

Special Topics

Although most of our writing groups are cross-disciplinary and specifically designed for people working on different kinds of writing, we have occasionally offered a special-topic writing group that followed the same basic model. One semester I worked with a colleague in microbiology to lead a graduate student group on science writing; another time I worked with a proposal-writing group that was cosponsored by our office of research and grants. My colleague Joan Hawthorne has led a cross-disciplinary case-writing group, as well as a faculty and grad student writing group in the College of Education and Human Development.

All these special-topic groups have required some modification of our basic structure and routine. If the group is small, it may not meet every week. If the group focuses on one type of writing, it may want to spend some of its time reading examples of that kind of writing. If the members are in a specialized field, the group may need co-leaders, one of whom would know more about the subject and the other about writing.

It's also possible for a general purpose group to decide to devote part of its time to a special topic. One group I was working with decided to spend a session on writing letters of recommendation. Everyone brought a recommendation they had written (with identifying information changed or deleted), and we read each other's letters and compared notes. In another group we realized that several of us were writing or editing newsletters for our departments or professional organizations. Bringing copies of our newsletters to the group enabled us to share ideas with each other and talk about what makes an effective newsletter.

Social and Collegial Aspects

Although it is possible for a group to work well together without becoming friends, we have found that the social aspects of our writing groups are as important as the work. In evaluations collected at the end of a new group's first semester, faculty always report that they have enjoyed getting to know people in other disciplines in a more relaxed and collegial setting than the typical department or committee meeting.

To some extent the social aspects develop naturally as the group goes along. People learn to joke with each other, to bring food to pass around, to make time for occasional "digressions" onto topics having to do with our families, current events, or campus politics. With continuing groups there usually comes a time when someone suggests getting off campus and having a purely social gathering such as a pot-luck dinner at someone's house or a Friday afternoon at a nearby pub. One group that called itself "The Writing Group That Wouldn't Die" had regular reunion meetings at the end of every semester, and those who had dropped out of the group for some reason were invited back for a celebratory drink.

In some cases the social aspects of these groups may be more important than the writing, especially for faculty who are new to campus or who feel isolated or alienated from their own departments. But the social aspects also help us work better together. Once we have shared a pot-luck dinner, it is easier to be honest with each other, and that is a key component of any successful group.

Benefits of Participating

When I was working on this book project, I asked my own writing group to review this section and to add comments of their own about the benefits of working with a writing group. Here is what some of them had to say:

> "It stretches the mind to read work from other disciplines—gets us out of our normal routine."

> "The obligation to others makes us more likely to get work done."

> "The synergy in an effective group can become very powerful."

> "It's a valuable experience if you are asked to review articles for professional journals."

> "This is one of the few places I get to hear about nonscience disciplines."

> "You benefit so much more than from just the one day your paper is read."

> "The intellectual stimulation is wonderful!"

> "Even on days when I was a slacker and didn't get the piece read, I wanted to come to the group. It's always interesting to hear what people say."

> "We end up discussing not just the paper but writing-related issues and other tangents, like the structure of different disciplines."

> "I've never once come away without being surprised by someone's idea."

Although these comments were culled from just one group—in this case a particularly successful, long-running group—they are very similar to the comments we hear from every group. It may not happen in every group, or even in every meeting of a successful group, but as one member of our group said, "Something definitely *happens* in a group that is working well."

Appendix B:
Sample Book Proposal Guidelines

Jossey-Bass: Elements of a Good Book Plan

A good book plan generally contains the following information, which Jossey-Bass finds essential in evaluating a project for publication consideration:

1. *Need.* Why is the book being written? Why do people need help on the topic at this time? How is the topic of increasing rather than passing or declining importance?

2. *Purpose.* What is the book designed to accomplish? How does it meet the need you have identified?

3. *Contribution.* What new is offered? In what ways would the book add to current knowledge and practice?

4. *Related and Competing Books.* Please list the author, title, and publisher of the main related and competing books; describe why they are not adequate to meet the need you have identified; and tell how your book would differ or be superior.

5. *Intended Audiences.* Be specific and describe the primary, secondary, and other audiences with respect to discipline, institutional affiliation, and position or title.

6. *Uses.* What would the book help the audiences to do, understand, improve, carry out, and so on? Distinguish between the

uses for the practitioner audiences and the uses for the academic audiences—or whatever distinction is most meaningful.

7. *Potential Textbook Adoption.* In addition to sales to individual practitioners and academics, Jossey-Bass books are often used as textbooks in college and university courses and corporate and government training courses. If your book would have such textbook use, please describe the level, titles, and average enrollment of courses for which it would be appropriate; the kinds and approximate number of institutions with such courses; and competing textbooks.

8. *Alternative Title Possibilities.* Along with your current working title, please suggest several alternative titles. We strive for titles that clearly communicate to all audiences the topic, purpose, and utility of books.

9. *Knowledge Base.* What is the research or experience base for the information in the book? Briefly describe any special studies or previous work relevant to this book.

10. *Outline of Contents and Chapter-by-Chapter Descriptions.* Provide a few sentences about the purpose and contents of each chapter, giving specific details and examples as well as general statements. Also explain the logic of the book's organization.

11. *Special Materials.* Briefly mention the purpose and approximate number of tables, figures, forms, supplements, appendices, and any other special materials to be included.

12. *Length.* How many double-spaced, typewritten pages do you anticipate the manuscript to be?

13. *Timetable.* What schedule is envisioned for preparing sample chapters (if not already included), the complete draft manuscript, and revisions of the manuscript?

14. *Sample Chapters.* Do not wait until the manuscript is completed to submit the plan. Instead, submit the plan with two or three sample chapters. If you would like some feedback be-

fore you prepare the sample chapters, send the plan without them, and we will offer an initial reaction. We prefer to learn of projects in their early stages to point out potential problems and offer editorial suggestions. If you would like us to return any of the materials you submit, please enclose a self-addressed, stamped envelope.

15. *Other Publishers.* Has the manuscript been sent to other publishers for consideration? If so, which ones? Note that Jossey-Bass has no objection to your informing other publishers that we are considering the plan.

16. *Background Information.* Please attach your vita, resume, or biography detailing your professional and educational background, including prior publications.

Appendix C:
A Few Good Books on Writing

In the Preface I alluded to the difficulty I sometimes have coming up with titles to recommend to colleagues who ask for "a good book on writing." The following are some that I do recommend, depending on what my colleagues are seeking.

I've made no attempt to be exhaustive here. There are no doubt others I could have mentioned. But these are the books I have learned from as a writer and teacher of writing and the ones I most frequently recommend to others.

Books I Recommend

Becker, H. S. *Writing for Social Scientists: How to Start and Finish Your Thesis, Book or Article* (Chicago Guides to Writing, Editing and Publishing). Chicago: University of Chicago Press, 1986.

This book is one of the classics. If more social scientists took Becker's advice, more people would enjoy reading social science. Also useful for qualitative researchers in all fields.

Day, R. A. *How to Write and Publish a Scientific Paper.* (5th ed.) Phoenix: Oryx Press, 1998.

An excellent resource for understanding the structure of a scientific paper.

———————

Elbow, P. *Writing Without Teachers* (2nd ed.) and *Writing With Power.* (2nd ed.) New York: Oxford University Press, 1998.

Elbow is one of the wisest and most thoughtful writing teachers I know. These particular books, which derive from Elbow's own experience as a once-blocked academic writer, were written for a general audience and, though published several years ago, have recently been reissued with updates by the author.

———————

Lanham, R. *Revising Prose*. (4th ed.) New York: Longman, 2000.

One of the best practical books on improving style—a close second, in my view, to Joseph Williams' *Style* (see the Williams listing).

———————

Williams, J. *Style: Ten Lessons in Clarity and Grace*. (6th ed.) New York: Longman, 2000. (A shorter version of this book is available from the University of Chicago Press as part of its series, *Chicago Guides to Writing, Editing and Publishing*.)

The best book I know on style. A linguist by training, Williams doesn't just preach; he explains the principles he teaches. Readers who like analytical explanations will find the book interesting as well as useful. But you don't have to follow the analysis to profit from the many examples with which Williams illustrates his "lessons." And the passages to edit at the end of each chapter (sample solutions in the back) are fun to play with.

Books Others Have Recommended

Booth, W., Colombe, G., and Williams, J. *The Craft of Research.* Chicago: University of Chicago Press, 1995.

I first encountered this book when it was recommended highly by one of the reviewers of my manuscript. Although designed primarily for students, the book is based on sound rhetorical principles and makes good reading for experienced academics and professionals as well.

Boice, R. *Professors as Writers: A Self-Help Guide to Productive Writing.* Stillwater, Okla.: New Forums Press, 1990.

As its subtitle suggests, this book is designed for those who see themselves as blocked academic writers. Some may find the prescriptive tone off-putting; others will appreciate the "brief, programmatic framework."

McCloskey, D. *Economical Writing.* (2nd ed.) Prospect Height, Ill.: Waveland Press, 1999.

Although I learned of this book only recently, I am already recommending it as a more useful alternative to Strunk and White's popular *Elements of Style*. A well known and respected economist, McCloskey manages in only ninety-eight pages to give some very good, rhetorically sound advice for academics and professionals in all fields.

Miner, L. E., Miner, J. T., and Griffith, J. *Proposal Planning and Writing.* (2nd ed.) Phoenix: Oryx Press, 1998.

Grant proposals seem to be one of the most challenging genres for academics and professionals to master. This guide doesn't just dictate format; it deals with different kinds of proposals (foundation, corporate, and government), explains the purpose of the various parts of the proposal, gives lots of examples from a wide range of fields, and offers critiques and reasons for rejection of sample proposals.

Moxley, J. *Publish, Don't Perish: The Scholar's Guide to Academic Writing and Publishing*. New York: Praeger, 1992.

This practical "how-to" book offers brief descriptions of various kinds of academic writing (for example, informative abstracts, book proposals), as well as general advice on such topics as "how to submit and market your work" and "how to revise and edit."

References

Booth, W. "The Rhetorical Stance." *College Composition and Communication*, 1963, *14*(3), 139–145.

Burke, K. *The Philosophy of Literary Form.* (3rd ed.) Berkeley: University of California Press, 1941; Regents of the University of California, 1973.

Day, R. *How to Write and Publish a Scientific Paper.* (5th ed.) Phoenix: Oryx Press, 1998.

Elbow, P. *Everyone Can Write: Essays Toward a Hopeful Theory of Writing and Teaching Writing.* New York: Oxford University Press, 2000.

Gere, A. *Writing Groups: History, Theory, and Implications.* Carbondale: Southern Illinois University Press, 1987.

Publication Manual of the American Psychological Association. (4th ed.) Washington, D.C.: American Psychological Association, 1994.

Rankin, E. "Changing the Hollow Conventions of Academic Writing." *Chronicle of Higher Education*, Apr. 4, 1998, p. A64.

Smith, F. *Writing and the Writer.* New York: Holt, Rinehart and Winston, 1982.

Williams, J. *Style: Ten Lessons in Clarity and Grace.* (6th ed.) Menlo Park, Calif.: Addison-Wesley, 1999.

Index